CLEAN PALEO

ONE-POT MEALS

100 Delicious Recipes from
Pan to Plate in 30 Minutes or Less

CHRISTINA SHOEMAKER
Creator of The Whole Cook

FAIR WINDS

Inspiring | Educating | Creating | Entertaining

Brimming with creative inspiration, how-to projects, and useful information to enrich your everyday life, Quarto Knows is a favorite destination for those pursuing their interests and passions. Visit our site and dig deeper with our books into your area of interest: Quarto Creates, Quarto Cooks, Quarto Homes, Quarto Lives, Quarto Drives, Quarto Explores, Quarto Gifts, or Quarto Kids.

First Published in 2020 by Fair Winds Press, an imprint of The Quarto Group,
100 Cummings Center, Suite 265-D, Beverly, MA 01915, USA.
T (978) 282-9590 F (978) 283-2742 QuartoKnows.com

Fair Winds Press titles are also available at discount for retail, wholesale, promotional, and bulk purchase. For details, contact the Special Sales Manager by email at specialsales@quarto.com or by mail at The Quarto Group, Attn: Special Sales Manager, 100 Cummings Center, Suite 265-D, Beverly, MA 01915, USA.

24 23 22 21 20   1 2 3 4 5

ISBN: 978-1-59233-969-3

Digital edition published in 2020
eISBN: 978-1-63159-904-0

Library of Congress Cataloging-in-Publication Data

Names: Shoemaker, Christina, author.
Title: Clean paleo one-pot meals : 100 delicious recipes from pan to plate
   in 30 minutes or less / Christina Shoemaker.
Description: Beverly, MA : Fair Winds Press, an imprint of The Quarto
   Group, 2020. | Includes index. | Summary: "In Clean Paleo One-Pot Meals,
   popular blogger Christina Shoemaker of The Whole Cook presents 100 quick
   and delicious recipes that go right from pan to plate"-- Provided by
   publisher.
Identifiers: LCCN 2020012710 | ISBN 9781592339693 (trade paperback) | ISBN
   9781631599040 (ebook)
Subjects: LCSH: Cooking (Natural foods) | One-dish meals. | High-protein
   diet--Recipes. | Prehistoric peoples--Nutrition. | LCGFT: Cookbooks.
Classification: LCC TX741 .S552 2020 | DDC 641.5/637--dc23
LC record available at https://lccn.loc.gov/2020012710a

Design: Samantha J. Bednarek
Cover Image: Christina Shoemaker
Page Layout: Samantha J. Bednarek
Photography: Christina Shoemaker and Meredith Brown on pages 9, 14, 25, and 186.

Printed in China

The information in this book is for educational purposes only. It is not intended to replace the advice of a physician or medical practitioner. Please see your health-care provider before beginning any new health program.

dedication

To Wyatt and Maddie—who always make me laugh
and challenge me to add more chocolate.
You're my very favorite humans.

contents

introduction

I am a food lover. If you know me at all, you know this to be true. I wake up thinking about what to eat, and by the time I've finished any meal, I'm planning my next.

My grandmother used to say I was like a bird because when I was small, I'd stand at her feet in her tiny white kitchen with my mouth open, ready for her to drop something in. Not much has changed.

While I was always someone who loved to eat, I was not always confident in the kitchen. And I most certainly wasn't making healthy food choices. In my twenties, I relied heavily on prepackaged microwave dinners and fast-food chain restaurants to keep me fed. If it was fried (and came with fries), I wanted it. I also had a six-pack-a-day soft drink habit and consumed copious amounts of vending machine snacks for breakfast at work each morning.

It wasn't until I became a mother that I developed any interest in cooking. All of a sudden, I was responsible for what food went into my children's growing bodies. Talk about pressure! I may not have known much about nutrition, but I most certainly knew that fast-food burgers and fries were not what they needed.

So, I started asking questions, reading books, and searching the Internet to better understand what the heck this whole clean eating thing was about. I was hooked right away. The idea of focusing on whole-food ingredients and limiting processed foods made complete sense to me. It just clicked.

I became an enthusiastic home cook, preparing every meal for my family and experimenting with ingredients I hadn't worked with before. My confidence in the kitchen skyrocketed. I could do this! I could prepare wholesome dishes for my children and husband—and they actually liked them!

As my confidence grew, I started documenting our meals each day on my Instagram account. I'd snap quick photos on my phone, unconvinced that anyone would be interested. Boy, was I wrong! There was tons of interest! I loved connecting with other people on there who were also pursuing a healthier lifestyle.

It wasn't long before the idea of a blog popped up. What if I had a place to share my recipes instead of just the pretty pictures of them? (Okay, those photos were not pretty. They were grainy and dark. I should be clear about that.)

On that blog, *The Whole Cook*, I learned a lot about creating yummy recipes the whole family would enjoy. My own personal family of food critics thoroughly tested each one. And trust me, nobody is more skeptical of whatever meal is placed in front of her than my five-year-old daughter.

Since 2016, I've shared hundreds of delicious recipes as The Whole Cook, and my top performers are always the 30-minute meals. Whether it's in a skillet, baking dish, single pot on the stove, or on a sheet pan in the oven, these recipes are the dishes that get made, shared, and raved about. And now with this cookbook, I'm bringing you 100 of my very favorites. Hopefully, they'll become your favorites too.

My blog readers have made it clear what they're looking for and why.

people want to feed their families healthy food but feel overwhelmed by it.

When dinnertime arrives, they are out of time, uninspired, and ready to just be done with the day. All those big Pinterest plans have flown out the window. Who has time (or the desire!) to stand in a hot kitchen chopping, simmering, and then cleaning for two hours? No, ma'am. Count me out on all of that.

I want to do as little as possible in the kitchen and still create a nutritious meal for my family.

fast food doesn't have to be junk food.

There's just something immensely satisfying about tossing all the ingredients on a sheet pan and letting everything roast. A few minutes after popping the pan in the oven, that incredible aroma fills the kitchen. Does June Cleaver live here? Nope. But she could.

You feel like Ina Garten when you pull that finished pan from the oven, but alas, you didn't have to hike the Alps to gather your ingredients or spend hours doing prep. Does it taste like you did? Indeed, it does.

This cookbook isn't for the Ina Gartens of the world. This cookbook is for those of us who want to feel like her in only 30 minutes. Those people are my people.

healthy food doesn't have to be complicated or weird.

The problem with so many good-for-you dishes (no matter how much time they take to make) is that often they come off as a little strange. A little *too* good for you.

Sure, you could swap a dehydrated kale wrap for a tortilla, but do you really want to?

Yes, you could prepare a pitcher of raw spinach, cucumber, and ginger juice to sip on every day, but again, do you want to?

I'm not alone when I say there is no way on God's green earth my family would be on board with any of those healthy solutions.

we want to eat healthy without it tasting like a punishment.

A healthy chili should still look and taste like the chili of your childhood. A stir-fry should taste *better* than takeout and not like a poor substitute.

My recipes are popular because they taste good while still being good for you.

The dishes you'll find in *Clean Paleo One-Pot Meals* are simple but flavorful; impressive but fast and easy; and perfect for the busy parent feeding a family or the individual who wants to meal prep for the week.

I'm so excited to share these recipes with you and can't wait for you to give them a try. I look forward to hearing how you incorporate them into your mealtime routine!

recipe icon key

Each recipe has one or more of the following icons for quick reference.

ICON	TERMINOLOGY	DEFINITION
	Dairy-free	These recipes do not contain the milk from mammals (such as cows or goats) or any food products made from milk.
	Egg-free	These recipes do not contain any eggs or any egg by-products.
	Vegetarian	These recipes do not contain meat but may include ingredients made from animal by-products such as eggs, honey, or ghee.
	Vegan	These recipes do not contain meat or any ingredients made from animal by-products such as eggs, honey, or ghee. Some recipes with this icon have a vegan-friendly alternative included.
	Keto	These recipes include ingredients that are lower in carbohydrates and are perfect for a low-carb diet.

1

the basics

When I first set out to adopt a healthier way of eating, I was afraid it would be too limiting. I feared a future of boiled chicken, egg whites, and kale. I can't even begin to stress how much I dislike the idea of eating huge quantities of kale. Gag. It would be my nightmare come to life.

And eating that kind of bland food just isn't sustainable. I can't do it. I love food too much! I want it to taste good while also making my body feel its very best. Is that too much to ask?

No, friend, it's not.

My other worry as I began transforming my family's eating habits was that it was going to take too much time. Now, I happen to love being in the kitchen. This should come as no surprise, since I voluntarily create recipes for my blog every single week. But when it's dinnertime, I'm ready to get out of that kitchen. Sound familiar? I want to be lying horizontal with a book or playing a card game with my sassy five-year-old and hilarious nine-year-old. I do not want to be creating a giant mess and then cleaning up said giant mess while everyone else sits around relaxing. Hard pass.

So, let's make eating healthy approachable.

the clean paleo approach

What's the big picture?

I don't like to label what we eat as good or bad. I believe that kind of thinking is a slippery slope and can create an unhealthy relationship with food. But does that mean all food is created equal? Well, no. Not even close.

Some foods are simply more nutritious for us than others. They fuel us, giving us more energy, and even help us get better rest at night.

And some foods don't have much nutritional value at all. They can fill our tummies for a little bit but make us feel sluggish and tired. We function better and we feel better when we limit those types of things. Recognizing that is the first step in making real, positive changes.

How you change your eating habits is completely up to you. Your answer may very well be different from mine, and that's okay! My goal is to arm you with quick, healthy recipes so it's easy for you and your family to eat well.

So What the Heck Is Paleo?

I have great news for you. There's no need to grab that bow and arrow or till the field for seed planting. Cleaning up your diet doesn't have to be complicated.

Let's dig in to what Clean Paleo means.

Unfortunately, you may very well come across some conflicting information out there about which foods are considered Paleo. It's totally okay. I like to keep things very simple.

If you're sticking to the most straight-forward definition (which I am), Paleo means noshing on a diet of quality whole foods. We're talking about the unprocessed eats here. Let's focus on nutrient-dense, vitamin-packed foods wherever possible. They should make our bodies stronger, our brains sharper, and our sleep more restful.

It seems like common sense, right? Well *of course* we want to eat what makes us healthier. But, as you know, this is actually a drastically different approach than our current Western diet, which is heavily processed, loaded with preservatives, and includes an astonishingly high number of ingredients that are possibly linked to various illnesses. Many folks see a correlation between the foods of today and the dramatic rise in chronic illness and obesity. We also tend to have more stress, more inflammation, and get less sleep. Now, genetics, environment, and lifestyle play a big role too, but nobody disputes that the food we put into our bodies is a factor worthy of examination. It's why there's such a growing interest in the clean eating movement.

i'm in! so, what can i eat?

Oh, so much good food!

But before we go further, let me make this disclaimer: THIS IS YOUR DIET. It's not my diet, your friend's diet, or the diet of that woman in the gym wearing the neon-green full-body spandex. You should make the choices that make the most sense for you. Period. I'm going to explain what a Paleo-inspired diet can look like, but take what you want from it.

If you're wanting to hear from someone who is rigid in their commitment to kale, I am not for you. Looking for someone who doesn't fill their home with Christmas cookies in December? I am not your gal. Pass me all the cookies. But

someone who carefully chooses healthy foods 85 percent of the time and believes in balance? Oh look, that's me!

Disclaimer over. Back to your question.

A Paleo-inspired diet includes lots of lean meat, poultry, seafood, vegetables, fruit, nuts, seeds, and healthy fats. Phew. Doesn't sound terrible, right? Plus, throw in plenty of dried herbs and spices for flavor. (I assure you I don't eat bland food. Ever.) There are even great sweeteners to play around with and a wide assortment of Paleo flours for baking. See? All good things.

I promise there is no shortage of good-for-you and totally delicious grub that fits perfectly in the Paleo-inspired diet.

Meat, Poultry, and Seafood

Select wild-caught seafood wherever possible. Let's pick on salmon for a minute to understand why. Farmed salmon is fed a processed feed that's higher in fat in order to yield very big fish. This dramatically changes the nutritional content of the salmon you eat. Not only does farmed salmon have more calories, fat, and sodium than wild salmon, but various studies indicate that farmed salmon also contain more *toxins* and *contaminants* than wild salmon. Toxins are scary. So, go wild, friends.

When purchasing meat, try to stick to grass-fed and organic wherever possible. It's not always an option, especially when eating out or if you find your grocery store offerings to be particularly limiting, but when available, it's the better way to go. The same goes for poultry.

Eggs

I can think of 100,000 ways to prepare eggs. They're so incredibly versatile! They're also easy to make and affordable. But which eggs to buy? Organic is always your best bet. When it comes to how the birds are cared for, pay special attention to pasture raised or free range. The chickens producing these eggs have some room to roam and forage for bugs. I like to think this leads to happier chickens and perhaps better eggs. Score!

Vegetables & Fruits

I eat my weight in veggies every day, and if you think that's an exaggeration . . . well, you're obviously right. But I do really love my veggies. That's what I'm getting at.

Organic veggies and fruits are ideal because we can avoid those unwelcome pesticides. Buying fresh produce in season and staying stocked up with frozen or canned options (always unsweetened and in natural juices) will help save money.

Fats

Want to add a bit of crunch to a salad or stir-fry? Need a quick snack? Nuts and seeds are the perfect solution. Honestly, there isn't much in this world that I enjoy more than a spoonful (or four) of almond butter.

Other amazing fats to include in your diet are extra-virgin olive oil, avocado oil, sesame oil, walnut oil, macadamia nut oil, coconut oil, and ghee. That's not an exhaustive list, but those are the main ones. When you see "cooking fat of choice" listed as an ingredient in a recipe here, those are the ones I'm referring to. Take your pick!

Flours

If you enjoy baked goods or want to thicken a sauce or soup, there are some fantastic flours I encourage you to try. My favorites are almond flour, arrowroot flour, coconut flour, tapioca flour, and Paleo flour (which is basically a premade blend of some of the others mentioned). These options are delicious, but not exactly the same as highly processed white flour. They're gluten free, brown more quickly, can have a slightly different texture, and are minimally processed. You can really create some fun dishes with these once you get used to how to work with them. (Don't worry—I'll show you!)

Sweeteners

Raw honey, maple syrup, coconut sugar, Medjool dates or date syrup (if made of 100 percent dates), and fruit juices are phenomenal sweeteners you can use in beverages, sauces, baked goods, and more. While you don't want to go crazy and guzzle a lot of the stuff, you can happily incorporate them into your healthy lifestyle. Just keep in mind that natural sugar is still sugar, so be conscious of your intake.

Vinegar

Vinegar is highly underrated as a way to maximize flavor. I personally love it to transform soups, sauces, and salad dressings. White, red wine, white wine, balsamic, apple cider, and rice vinegars are all fair game. Remember that a little goes a long way because they pack a punch!

what to avoid?

We've covered all the delicious foods we can enjoy on a Paleo-inspired diet, but let's discuss what you may want to consider avoiding and why.

Refined and Added Sugars

Sugar occurs naturally in any food that contains carbohydrates, so nobody is suggesting that we completely eliminate it in all forms. Instead, how about we focus on *added* sugar? When you start reading food labels, you'll be surprised by how many packages list sugar (or sucrose, high-fructose corn syrup, dextrose, or malt syrup) as an ingredient. That's added sugar. That's different than the naturally occurring sugar found in foods.

So why do companies add it to so much? The obvious answer is to sweeten the product, but sometimes, it's simply to change the texture or extend the shelf life. We consume so much of this added sugar without even realizing it (because we're definitely not paying attention) that we end up with way more in our diet than is good for us. And, we're oblivious to it!

So, pay attention. Step out of the dark, friend. Read your labels. Skip or limit the added sugar.

Grains

This is a tough one for lots of people. A standard Paleo diet does not include wheat, barley, rice, corn, oats, or quinoa. But don't sweat it! You can re-create lots of the traditionally gluten-filled fare with gluten-free Paleo ingredients!

Legumes

Beans, peanuts, lentils, and soy are typically avoided because of the high amount of lectins and phytic acid they contain, which may be linked to leaky gut (doesn't that sound pleasant?). A ban on soy includes edamame, tofu, and tempeh, and once you start reading labels, you're going to see that soy is added to almost *everything*. But wait! There are some yummy legumes you can still munch on. Green beans, snow peas, and sugar snap peas are all good to go!

That said, there is a second perspective that feels consuming legumes in small doses may be worthwhile. They're low in fat and high in fiber, protein, and iron. Soaking and cooking the legumes may deactivate most of the lectins and drastically decrease the amount of phytic acid. The choice is yours.

Vegetable Oils

These oils are highly processed because the types of oils in this category come from plants that really make you work for their oil. Examples include soybean oil, corn oil, rice bran oil, sunflower oil, safflower oil, peanut oil, cottonseed oil, and canola oil. (Imagine trying to make oil from a kernel of corn or a sunflower seed. It would take some work! Whereas olives, avocado, and coconut can yield plenty of oil with minimal processing because they contain plenty of fat.) And hey, there are an abundance of awesome oils available to us that just plain work better!

Highly Processed Foods

Processed foods generally include many of the things listed here to avoid, especially grains (hello, white flour!), added sugars, and hydrogenated vegetable oils. They're also designed to make you want to eat more, so it's easy to overindulge.

Keep things simple. Choose quality whole foods with minimal processing. If an ingredient label is full of items you can't pronounce, it's likely something that would fall in the highly processed food category.

and now the confusing foods

The good and the bad are fairly cut-and-dried, but there are a few foods that are often debated in the Paleo community. Those conversations can create a ton of confusion. Do you eat it or not? Maybe. That choice is yours.

Do a little personal experimentation, friend. I suggest sticking to a strictly Paleo diet for 30 days. See how you feel. Then, if there are a few things you're wanting to try again, do that. How does your body respond? Do your research and decide for yourself.

Potatoes

The biggest concerns regarding white potatoes are a) they're starchy, b) they have a high glycemic index, c) it's very easy to overindulge in them, and d) they're all too often used in highly processed and completely unhealthy ways. I concede all of these points. However, I recognize all the complex carbohydrates, antioxidants, dietary fiber, potassium, and other nutrients that potatoes give us. They can actually help our bodies fight inflammation! So, does my family eat potatoes? Yes, we do. But I am sure to prepare them in healthy ways and in moderation.

Since the general consensus is that sweet potatoes are the healthiest option in the potato family, I've included them in several recipes in this cookbook. If you prefer to swap it for another potato, go for it. If you want to skip the sweet potatoes completely and use other veggies that requires a similar cooking time, such as green beans, carrots, or butternut squash, go for it.

Decide on the Big Potato Issue for yourself. Know that whatever you choose is great!

Dairy

Oh dairy, you complicated beast.

The vast majority of Paleo or clean eating advocates say dairy is a no. The milk sugar *lactose* is not well tolerated in many people, the milk protein *casein* can harm your gut lining, and there's some talk that milk may increase your risk of certain cancers.

The widely accepted exception to the no-dairy rule is ghee—glorious, delicious ghee. You'll see it in many of my recipes, both here and on my blog. What is it? Oh, friend, if you're new to ghee I'm going to change your life. Ghee has actually been around forever, originating in ancient Indian cooking. It is butter that's slowly simmered until it separates into liquid fat and milk solids. When those milk solids are removed, it's nearly lactose free and casein free! (It also makes it ideal for frying because there are no solids left to burn.) There's growing evidence that there are health benefits to eating ghee, which is wonderful news for this ghee lover. And my husband, who has a mighty powerful dairy allergy, can consume ghee with no issues! (To all of you with dairy allergies, I'm not saying to try it for yourself. Talk to your doctor. I'm just a woman with a blog and a kitchen.)

getting started

Before we jump into the recipes, let's chat about how to kick off a healthy lifestyle for you and your family.

Articulate Your Goals

Take a quick minute and think about what you want to accomplish here. Are you looking to incorporate one healthy meal into your day each day? That's awesome. Or, are you jumping in and transforming your diet from breakfast to dinner? Sounds great! Both answers are valid. Think about which path feels like the right one for you and your family.

Celebrate Positive Changes, No Matter How Small

The #1 recommendation I give people who ask how to start transforming their diet is this one. Celebrate every change, my friend! If you make one healthy swap each day, that's a victory! Treat it like one.

Don't look at the person who works out for two hours a day and make that the standard by which you'll measure yourself. You may not be that person! Look at you and what you're doing right instead of focusing on what someone else is doing. This is your journey, after all!

For example, you might begin by tackling your dinnertime routine. Instead of picking up fast food on your way home from work three nights a week, you start cooking recipes from this cookbook for those three nights. That's a great place to begin and worth celebrating! (Take a peek at chapter 2 for ideas on how to meal prep, so those meals will be just as easy as going through the drive-thru.)

Wherever you are in your health journey, recognize that we're not all starting in the same place. We have different schedules, incomes, family situations, and so much more. Work with what you have and honor each positive change.

Create a Kitchen That Supports Your Goals

If my kitchen is filled with jalapeño-flavored kettle potato chips, I'm going to eat them. It's just a fact. If it's 7 p.m. and I haven't started dinner, then all bets are off, and I'll demolish that bag of chips in 15 minutes. I know this about myself, so I choose to keep that ridiculously tasty snack out of my kitchen. Does this mean I never have them? Heck no. If I really want them, I'll get in the car, drive to the grocery store, and purchase them. I'm totally good with that. In that instance, I've made a conscious decision to eat those chips, and that's fine by me! I just don't want to set myself up for a situation where it's too convenient to pass them up. I want the foods that make me feel my best to be readily available and convenient. That means you'll find very few processed foods in my house.

My recommendation is to rid your kitchen of the things you want to limit and instead set yourself up to build healthy habits! Stay stocked up on whole foods, real ingredients, and fast healthy meal solutions. Keep that refrigerator overflowing with high-quality protein, fruits, and vegetables. Fill the pantry with staples that are in line with the lifestyle you want to have.

When your kitchen is bursting with nourishing food, you're far more inclined to eat nourishing food.

Build a Support System

We are more likely to succeed when we have a support system in place that reinforces our commitment to healthy eating.

Is your family on board with what you're trying to do? When I first started down this path, my husband was a skeptic. The guy survived on a diet of mostly fried chicken and potatoes, so he was understandably less than enthusiastic about making changes. I didn't let that stop me, though. I set out to prove that I could make the comfort foods he loved using better ingredients. And I have! That same man now raves about cauliflower rice. So, if you have family members who aren't thrilled about the idea of zoodles, it's okay. Win them over one recipe at a time. (Psst! This cookbook will help with that!)

When trying to sway the doubters, here's an important tip: Don't talk about how good for them the food you're preparing is. Zip those lips and let the taste of the food do the talking for you! If I had told my husband that a particular casserole was dairy free (back before he developed his dairy allergy, thanks to a tick bite), he would have been looking for what was weird about it in every bite. Of course, the same is absolutely true for my children. My daughter once declared that her applesauce was too spicy. *Applesauce*. You get what I'm saying, though. The trick is to just let people enjoy the food without trying to sell them on the food. If it tastes good, they'll love it, no matter what sorcery you performed in the kitchen.

If your family and friends are already ready to encourage you on your journey, that is awesome! You have a support system to help you stick to these positive changes. So use it! Talk to them. Tell them what you're doing, what new ingredients you're trying, or what snacking swaps you've made.

Stop Beating Yourself Up

We can really be our own worst enemies, can't we? Think about it. Is anyone harder on you than you? When I'm ready for bed at night, my brain loves to decide that's the right time to evaluate all my life decisions.

That self-sabotage shows up in our diets too. We eat an entire bag of jalapeño-flavored kettle potato chips (just me?) or chocolate chip morsels that we hide on the top shelf of the pantry (again, just me?), then decide to give up on all healthy eating because we "ruined it already."

Just stop.

Eat the bag of chips and move on. Enjoy devouring the chocolate morsels and let it go. It's not going to keep you from your goals. It's a bag of chips. It's okay. You're okay. It's just food and it's just one snack (or meal or day or week). Keep it moving.

Do It

The hardest part is starting. That's true for everything, isn't it? But you've got this. So, let's do this, one easy meal at a time.

Here's the big message I want to share with you. It's not all or nothing. If you want to make changes, do that. Every change, no matter how small, is an important change!

2

meal prep 101

Having your meals prepped for the
week is insanely satisfying. It's right up there
with watching a barista make latte art or
getting sucked into one of those viral
soap-cutting videos. You know what
I'm talking about, right? It's not just me?

why meal prep?

We're more likely to make healthy decisions when the food is already prepared and available to eat. When 5 p.m. hits and I haven't even thought about dinner, I'm ready to call it quits before I even start. Peeling a bunch of carrots and trying to come up with a way to make chicken taste special is the last thing I want to do at that point. But if I've taken the time to do it ahead of time (perhaps on a Sunday afternoon with some good music blasting in my kitchen), I can quickly pull together a healthy dinner any night of the week in just a few minutes.

You can save money by purchasing the groceries you need in bulk. If you know you'll use a total of 3 pounds (1.4 kg) of chicken that week, it's typically less expensive to buy a 3-pound (1.4 kg) package versus buying three 1-pound (455 g) packages. Additionally, if you make your lunches for the week ahead of time, you're less likely to hit that drive-thru when 1 p.m. hits and you suddenly realize you never took a lunch break.

My time is precious. How about yours? Do you have hours to spare with nothing to do? Yeah, I didn't think so. Investing some time in your meal prep one afternoon (or evening or morning or whatever works best for you) saves so much time in the rest of your week. You are only making one trip to the grocery store (a major time-saver right there). And when you're cooking, you're in the zone and making the most of that time. You confidently move through the kitchen from one dish to another like you're Bobby Flay battling it out on *Iron Chef*.

Oh, that dinner stress can hit hard at 5 p.m. when you realize you have to come up with dinner on the fly, doesn't it? Meal prep greatly reduces stress because dinner is never a mystery and the work is already done! What a time to be alive! No really. Eliminating that holy-crap-what-am-I-making-and-why-is-everyone-expecting-me-to-cook-anyway dread is a beautiful thing.

before you begin

Make sure you have storage containers to hold all that glorious food you'll be making. You'll want a variety of sizes to accommodate everything, including soups, casseroles, entrees, sauces, and sides. Popular containers are often made from stainless steel, glass, or BPA-free plastic. Will you be reheating food in the same containers you store it in? If so, then make sure the container you choose can handle the heat. Are you planning to take lunches to work? You might want containers that have separate compartments for each part of your meal.

The Weekly Routine

Consider what your week looks like. Most people choose to meal plan for the next five days instead of the full seven days in a week. (Food tends to go bad in five days or less.) What do your next five days look like? Do your kids have sports that might keep the family out late for two of those evenings? Perhaps a portable dinner would work best so everyone can eat at the ballfields. Is it your turn to host book club and you have to feed a crowd? A soup would be an easy solution.

1. Plan your meals. Peruse your favorite cookbooks, blogs, Instagram feed, and Pinterest accounts for recipe inspiration. What looks good to you? Ask the family what they're craving.

2. Make a shopping list. Don't walk into that grocery store without a plan. See what ingredients you already have and write down everything you want to purchase. This small task ensures you won't forget anything and makes the most of your time in the store.

3. Spend one day each week tackling the grocery shopping and prepping your delicious meals and snacks. Pick the day of the week that's best for you. For most people, it's Saturday or Sunday, but it really depends on your schedule.

mistakes to avoid

If you're new to meal prep, you may feel tempted to jump right in with both feet and prepare enough food to satisfy an army. Before you take the leap, learn from my mistakes. These tips will help you maximize your time and avoid having to toss a ton of uneaten food by week's end.

Don't overextend yourself.
Are you really going to need five different dinner recipes plus five different lunches? Likely no. Plan ahead for the meals you may eat out and when leftovers can be used for the next day's lunch. It will save you time, stress, and food waste!

Likewise, don't choose too many complicated recipes at one time.
If you're looking at this week's recipe inspiration and one entree has a lot of steps, keep the other recipes extra simple. You'll be so glad you did! It makes your prep day far less stressful.

Don't make food you won't actually eat.
Man, I really wish I loved kale. I wish it was my favorite food in all the world instead of what I loathe the most. But that's not my reality. So, if in an effort to become a kale lover, I make five gorgeous kale dishes that I know in my heart of hearts I won't touch, all that meal prep time was wasted. There are plenty of healthy foods we do want to eat, so let's not waste our time and money on foods that don't excite us. Find something you'll be happy to devour!

Don't use the same cooking method for everything.
Don't pick all stovetop recipes for your meal prep day or you'll waste time waiting for an available burner. I like to have a few things simmering on the stove, another something in the oven, a soup in the slow cooker, and a stew in the Instant Pot. Boom. That's called maximizing your kitchen, my friend!

Similarly, don't use the same pot or pan for everything.
You'll get so much more done if you're not waiting for that one pan to be available again.

And don't forget to set timers.
This is especially important if you're cooking multiple recipes at one time. I know you think you'll remember that the sheet-pan meal has to come out of the oven in 20 minutes, but what if you're busy stirring a sauce on the stove and forget? Better to set a timer for each recipe so nothing burns. I usually have several timers going on my phone at one time. It works like a charm!

Don't cook more food than you can store.
What's your refrigerator space like? Do you have space for only a few days' worth of meals? That's fine! Just keep that in mind when planning what you want to make.

But don't forget the freezer.

When most people think of meal prep, they're imagining all the ways they'll fill the fridge. But what about the freezer? My freezer currently looks like I'm readying the family for Armageddon. I kid you not. We have enough meals in there to keep us fed for the next month. Now, that may be a bit overboard, but I cannot tell you how reassuring it is to know I can refuse to cook dinner any night I want. I always have good food in there just waiting to be reheated!

Don't make too little food.

You know the size of your family and the size of their appetites. A recipe may say it feeds four, but if your nine-year-old son has the appetite of two grown men (mine does), then it may not be enough food. Double that recipe if you need to! It's usually easy to do and, hey, if you end up with too much, you can always freeze it.

Don't forget snacks and sides.

Meal prep isn't just for entrees! Sides and snacks are so easy to prepare and guarantee you really have everything you need for a full day of healthy eating. Mindless snacking on vending machine offerings is a lot less appealing when you have options at your fingertips that will reinforce your commitment to healthy eating. I give some great ideas at the end of this chapter.

That's it! Now you're ready to meal prep, my friend!

HOW LONG WILL MEAL-PREP FOOD LAST BEFORE GOING BAD?

Many foods are good for three to five days if refrigerated in airtight containers. There are a few things, like fish, that only last for one or two days, so get familiar with the U.S. Food and Drug Administration recommendations for refrigerator and freezer storage when you start down the meal-prep path. You can find super helpful guides on their website. If you know that a particular recipe falls in that one- to two-day window, you'll want to eat that earlier in the week and save something from the three- to five-day window for a little later.

The FDA says that freezing foods can make them safe indefinitely, but they do have some timing recommendations in order to maintain the quality of the foods. This information can also be found on their website.

good-for-you paleo snacks

Are you feeling snacky? Me too, friend. Always.

Healthy snack options can give you more energy during the day and help you make better mealtime decisions too! I don't know about you, but if I'm feeling a bit starved and it's dinnertime, then I make less-than-stellar dinner choices. A hangry (hungry + angry = *hangry*) Christina is a monster who can demolish villages in pursuit of food, and that food is 100 percent not going to be food that fuels her body. That food will leave me lethargic and disappointed in myself. So, let's all avoid hangry Christina.

When I have healthy snacks available that are—and this is important—easy, I'm going to reach for them! The same rule applies to my kids. If apples are washed, and in the fridge, they'll devour them. But if we're out of apples, then my kids will eat whatever is available. My goal is to make sure those snack choices are good ones we can all feel great about.

While I keep an up-to-date list of my favorite good-for-you packaged snacks on my blog, let's explore some yummy and fast Paleo snack options you can make or have at home.

ants on a log
These are celery sticks topped with almond butter and raisins. Oh, my kids get excited for this one. Part of the fun is letting them assemble these themselves!

apple slices + nut butter
This is easily the snack I grab most often. There's just something so satisfying about combining the sweetness and crunch of the apple with the salty creaminess of that nut butter. Almond butter, cashew butter, and sunflower seed butter are all delicious solutions!

applesauce
It's not just for children! I remember the first time I tried it as an adult, I was surprised by how good it still was. The good news is that, while you can make it at home, it's surprisingly easy to find applesauce with no added sugar.

baby carrots wrapped in deli roast beef + mustard
This tastes like a sandwich (I swear it!), but it's bite size and portable enough to take on the go! Switch up your deli meat and condiment for lots of variations.

bacon
Who says bacon can't be a snack? Nobody I want to know. Find a high-quality, pastured, and responsibly raised bacon (we're an exclusively turkey-bacon household over here, but find a bacon you love). Cook it on a Saturday morning when you're making that big breakfast for the family and set aside a few slices for snacking.

bacon-wrapped dates
These are a perfect mix of sweet and savory! I recommend Medjool dates, as they're pretty big and won't get hard when you bake them. Wrap a third of a slice of bacon around each date and bake at 425°F (220°C, or gas mark 7) for 15 to 20 minutes. (If you use a thin bacon, you'll want to reduce that cooking time.)

banana topped with nut butter, raisins, and shredded coconut
This feels like a dessert, I kid you not. It's so rich and fun. And, it's perfect for both adults *and* children!

broccoli florets + ranch dressing

I know not everyone wants to chomp on fresh broccoli florets, but I swear if you dip them in ranch dressing, you'll get more excited for it. There are several Paleo brands available if you don't want to make the ranch dressing yourself.

carrot sticks

Not to sound totally boring, but I've become a big fan of carrot sticks in the last few years. It's my #1 favorite food to sneak into movie theaters. (Don't tell.) I also bring a big tub with me to my son's baseball games, and my daughter and I snack right through every inning!

chicken sausage

Choose a nitrate- and sugar-free chicken sausage. Sauté a few quickly in a skillet (or grill them if it's that time of year) and store them in the fridge for easy snacking.

cucumber slices

Bland? A little. But it's still a solid snack solution! They are very low in calories; have a hint of crunch; and are awesome for dipping in ranch dressing or eating alone!

dark chocolate

Try a high-quality dairy-free dark chocolate that's low in sugar. Find one that's at least 70 percent cacao. The flavor is rich and not overly bitter but could very well curb any chocolate cravings you're having.

deli meat

Enjoy a slice or two of your favorite organic, no-sugar-added deli meat when you need a quick bite. Have an extra few minutes? Wrap slices around strips of bell pepper, carrot sticks, or cucumber.

dried fruit

There are so many to choose from! Raisins, dates, and apricots are a few you'll have no problem finding without any added sugar. Others to look for are peaches, pears, strawberries, blueberries, and pineapple. Just check those ingredients!

fresh fruit

Most people know that fresh fruit is a healthy snack idea. The common complaint is that it can go bad before you consume it. That's a legitimate concern! The trick is to figure out which fruit you enjoy and keep plenty of that particular fruit on hand. For my family, that means we'll always have apples, oranges, strawberries, blueberries, grapes, peaches, pears, and bananas in our kitchen. I buy watermelon, pineapple, cantaloupe, and kiwi less often. While we love them, they require more preparation (cutting a watermelon is not how I want to spend 30 minutes of my life), so those have a tendency to go bad. The fruit your family enjoys may differ from ours. Just pick what works best for you!

I suggest storing your fruit where the kids can reach it. My kids know they can always grab an apple without asking, so they eat a lot of them! And I have to haul myself to the kitchen less often to get them snacks—a win for everyone!

frozen fruit

Pop your grapes in the freezer for a few hours, and I swear they taste like candy. There's just something about that texture change that makes them special! Or, whip up your frozen pineapple or banana in a high-powered blender and call it a sorbet!

guacamole + plantain chips or veggies

When I first transformed my diet, I think I ate this snack every single day for a solid year. I've since discovered plenty of other snacking options, but guacamole (with basically anything) will always remain a favorite. Make your own guacamole or stock your fridge with one of the many store-bought varieties available.

hard-boiled eggs

Packed with protein and easily stored in the refrigerator, hard-boiled eggs are always a great nutritious snack idea.

jerky or meat sticks

Jerky has come a long way in the last few years. There are so many brands making high-quality and very flavorful jerky, but always check those ingredients!

nuts

These include almonds, cashews, walnuts, pecans, and (my favorite) pistachios! There are so many options, and they're easy to find.

paleo granola

There are many great brands producing Paleo granola out there right now. They're flavored a thousand different ways and usually include a combination of nuts and seeds plus coconut, chocolate, or dried fruit. I have a seriously yummy recipe for Sheet-Pan Blueberry Granola on page 179!

paleo snack bars

Thanks to the growing popularity of healthy eating, there are plenty of delicious Paleo snack bars on the market now. Full of real-food ingredients and containing no added sugar, they're a super snack when you're on the go. Many are perfect for a Paleo (or just plain healthy) lifestyle.

paleo trail mix

Paleo trail mix is very similar to Paleo granola and will include ingredients like nuts, seeds, chocolate, and/or dried fruit. The big difference is that the pieces are larger and the taste is usually more savory than sweet. (Toss in some bits of jerky!)

plantain chips

I often use plantain chips as a vehicle for other things (guacamole, salsa, avocado dip, etc.), but there are some really tasty chips you'll likely enjoy without any dip at all.

salsa + plantain chips

Make your own salsa (it's easy!) or purchase one of the many varieties you can find at the store. The same goes for plantain chips! Just check the ingredients to ensure you're avoiding the things you want to avoid.

seeds

Roast your own pumpkin seeds for a fun snack option that you can flavor however you like. Give sunflower seeds a try when you have a hankering for something salty that you can buy at any grocery store.

tomato slices + sprinkle of salt

Keep your snacking simple with this one. That salt makes a big difference! I grew up watching my mom eat this all the time and never understood it. As an adult, I get it! It's so good!

vegetable chips

If you haven't tried veggie chips before, you may be surprised by all the yummy flavors out there! Peruse the chip aisle in your local natural foods store or the natural foods section of your supermarket, and you'll see some made from sweet potatoes, carrots, beets, and even green beans. They're crispy and salty! They are a perfect replacement for regular potato chips.

3

throw-together breakfast dishes

I never tire of breakfast food. How about you?
In fact, I believe breakfast shouldn't be limited to
that first meal of the day. I'll whip up a hash or
frittata for lunch or dinner when the craving hits!

Now, I know that mornings can get super busy. We're juggling a lot, whether it's getting ready for work or getting the kids dressed and out the door. A thoughtful breakfast is usually the first thing to go. That's where these easy breakfast recipes come in. They cook fast. They require minimal prep. They don't require any additional sides because we're cooking everything together to keep it super simple. Most can even be made in advance and enjoyed throughout the week!

For those of you who just aren't into eggs or have an egg allergy, I have options for you too! You can easily omit the eggs in all the hash recipes, and they will still be very hearty.

You should also check out my Sautéed Apples (page 173), Easy Fruit Bake (page 182), and Sheet-Pan Blueberry Granola (page 179). They're all perfect for an egg-free breakfast!

sheet-pan eggs in sweet potato hash

Keep breakfast simple with a tasty hash of sweet potato, onion, and baked eggs. You'll only need a few ingredients!

PREP TIME 5 minutes
TOTAL TIME 25 minutes
MAKES 4 servings

2 large sweet potatoes, cut into ½-inch (1 cm) cubes

½ large white or yellow onion, diced into ½-inch (1 cm) pieces

1½ teaspoons extra-virgin olive oil or coconut oil

4 large eggs

Salt

Handful of fresh herbs, chopped (basil, cilantro, or parsley work great)

1. Preheat the oven to 425°F (220°C, or gas mark 7).

2. Spread the sweet potatoes and onion in a single layer on a 9½ x 13-inch (24 x 33 cm) baking sheet. (This is a quarter sheet pan. While I typically recommend a 12 x 17-inch [30 x 43 cm] pan for most sheet-pan meals, the ingredients for this recipe won't take up much space, so a quarter pan is perfect.)

3. Drizzle the oil over the veggies. Give it all a quick stir. Spread in an even layer.

4. Bake for 15 minutes. Remove from the oven and stir. Spread again in an even layer.

5. Use a spatula to create four little spaces for your eggs. Crack one egg into each hole. Sprinkle salt on the eggs. Bake until the egg whites are set and the egg yolks are cooked to how you like them, 5 to 8 minutes.

6. Remove from the oven and sprinkle fresh herbs on top before serving.

sheet-pan steak & eggs

Growing up, I remember my dad getting so excited for steak and eggs whenever we'd eat out. As an adult, I understand what all the fuss was about. It's typically not something you want to make at home because preparing a steak can be quite a lot of work. We usually want our breakfasts to be quick! This sheet-pan breakfast solves that dilemma for you. Enjoy steak, eggs, and crispy broccoli for a very satisfying and impressive start to your day!

PREP TIME 5 minutes
TOTAL TIME 30 minutes
MAKES 3 to 4 servings

**12 ounces (340 g)
broccoli florets**

**2 tablespoons (28 ml)
extra-virgin olive oil**

**1 pound (455 g) top sirloin
steak, cut into strips ½ inch
(1 cm) thick and 3 to 4 inches
(7.5 to 10 cm) long**

¼ teaspoon garlic powder

**¼ teaspoon salt,
plus more to taste**

¼ teaspoon black pepper

6 to 8 large eggs

1. Preheat the oven to 425°F (220°C, or gas mark 7).

2. Place the broccoli on a 12 x 17-inch (30 x 43 cm) baking sheet and drizzle with the oil. Toss until coated and then spread in a single layer. Bake for 15 minutes (see Tip).

3. Remove from the oven. Mix the steak with the broccoli and then spread out on the baking sheet. Season with garlic powder, salt, and black pepper. Move the florets and steak around to create six to eight spaces for your eggs. Crack an egg into each hole and sprinkle with salt.

4. Bake until the egg whites are set and the egg yolks are cooked to how you like them, another 7 to 10 minutes. (Watch those eggs as they cook!)

TIP
- I love my roasted broccoli extra crispy, but if you prefer it less crispy, just reduce that initial broccoli cooking time from 15 minutes down to 12 minutes.

chicken sausage frittata

This fully loaded frittata is inspired by my all-time favorite breakfast casserole by a similar name, but it cooks even faster. It's packed with flavor thanks to the salsa whisked into the eggs, and the chicken sausage, spinach, and riced sweet potato.

PREP TIME 10 minutes
TOTAL TIME 30 minutes
MAKES 8 slices

2 tablespoons (28 ml) extra-virgin olive oil or (28 g) ghee (For dairy-free dishes, use extra-virgin olive oil.)

½ white or yellow onion, diced into ½-inch (1 cm) pieces

1 cup (about 5 ounces, or 140 g) riced or shredded sweet potato (see Tip)

9 large eggs

½ cup (130 g) salsa

½ teaspoon salt

½ teaspoon black pepper

1 packed cup (about half a 5-ounce, or 140 g, package) baby spinach

2 fully cooked chicken sausages, sliced ¼-inch (6 mm) thick (see Tip)

1. Preheat the oven to 425°F (220°C, or gas mark 7).

2. Add the oil or ghee, onion, and sweet potato to a cast-iron skillet over medium-high heat. Sauté until the onion is softened and the potato has some browning, stirring frequently, 3 to 5 minutes.

3. Meanwhile, whisk together the eggs, salsa, salt, and black pepper in a large bowl. Set aside.

4. When the onion is done, turn off the stove. Spread the onion and potato mixture across the bottom of the skillet so it is evenly distributed. Layer the spinach leaves on top and then layer on your chicken sausage. Pour your egg mixture over everything.

5. Bake until the center is just set, 18 to 20 minutes. Check to make sure the center isn't very wiggly and then remove from the oven. Let it rest for a few minutes before serving.

TIP

- I use chicken sausage that's gluten and casein free and has no added nitrates. Use whatever brand you like or even swap it out for beef or turkey sausage!

- I use frozen riced sweet potato. The only ingredient is sweet potato. I don't even thaw it before sautéing! You can also shred or rice your own sweet potato at home if you prefer.

spicy sausage & egg skillet

Use your favorite precooked sausage to create a flavorful egg scramble that packs some heat! Amp up the intensity with extra hot sauce in the eggs and a hefty dose of sriracha before serving.

PREP TIME 5 minutes
TOTAL TIME 15 minutes
MAKES 4 servings

3 tablespoons (42 g) ghee, divided (see Tip)

1 cup (70 g) sliced mushrooms

2 precooked sausages, sliced ¼ inch (6 mm) thick

1 teaspoon minced garlic

8 large eggs

1½ teaspoons hot sauce (see Tip)

¾ teaspoon salt

¼ teaspoon chipotle chile powder

Sriracha sauce

1. Add 2 tablespoons (28 g) of the ghee, the mushrooms, and the sausage to a large skillet over medium-high heat. Sauté until the mushrooms are soft and the sausage has some browning, 3 to 4 minutes. Add the garlic. Stir and give it a quick sauté, about 1 minute, to achieve a golden color.

2. Meanwhile, whisk together the eggs, ¼ cup (60 ml) water, hot sauce, salt, and chile powder in a medium bowl. (The water helps make the eggs a little more fluffy since we're not using milk.)

3. Reduce the heat to medium-low. Add the remaining 1 tablespoon (14 g) ghee to the skillet. Pour the egg mixture over the mushroom mixture. The eggs will begin cooking right away. Use a spatula to fold the cooked outer edges of the eggs toward the center. Do this repeatedly until you don't have any more liquid in the pan.

4. Serve topped with a hearty drizzle of your favorite sriracha sauce.

TIP

- You can easily substitute a different cooking fat for ghee if you're completely dairy free or just prefer an alternative. I use ghee because it's my absolute favorite for eggs!

- Check out the ingredients in your hot sauce and sriracha sauce.

fried eggs with sweet potato rounds

Sometimes, you don't need anything more than eggs and potatoes. This whole dish cooks in less than 15 minutes. It's perfect for two!

PREP TIME 5 minutes
TOTAL TIME 25 minutes
MAKES 2 servings

1 medium sweet potato, cut into ¼-inch (6 mm)-thick rounds

½ teaspoon salt, plus more to taste

½ teaspoon paprika

2 tablespoons (28 g) coconut oil

1 tablespoon (15 g) ghee (see Tip)

2 to 4 large eggs

Black pepper, to taste

1. In a large bowl, toss your potato rounds in the salt and paprika so they're well seasoned.

2. Add the oil to a large nonstick skillet over medium-high heat. Once hot, add half of the potato rounds. You should hear a sizzle when you add them to the skillet. Cook for 2½ to 4 minutes until the side touching the skillet has some browning. Flip and cook for another 2½ to 4 minutes. Remove the rounds from the skillet and place on a paper towel–lined plate.

3. Repeat with the remaining potato rounds. If you're low on oil, add another ½ tablespoon before doing the second half. All the potato rounds should be on the plate when finished.

4. Reduce the heat to medium and wipe out the skillet.

5. Add the ghee to the cleaned skillet. Once melted, crack the eggs on one side of the skillet and sprinkle with salt and black pepper. Place the potato rounds beside the eggs. Cover the skillet and cook until the egg whites are set and the egg yolks are cooked to how you like them, about 3 minutes.

TIP
• You can easily substitute a different cooking fat for ghee if you're completely dairy free or just prefer an alternative. I use ghee because it's my absolute favorite for eggs!

turkey bacon baked egg cups

Eggs and bacon are the two most essential breakfast items of all the essential breakfast items. Am I right? I'm right. So, let's bake them together! If you're new to cooking with turkey bacon, you'll quickly discover that there are some fantastic brands and some less fantastic brands. I really recommend the thick, minimally processed turkey bacon you'll find in the natural foods section of your grocery store. It's so much more delicious, it's better for you, and it will better replicate that pork bacon we all grew up loving.

PREP TIME 5 minutes
TOTAL TIME 27 minutes
MAKES 12 egg cups

1½ to 2 tablespoons (23 to 28 ml) extra-virgin olive oil

12 slices turkey bacon, halved crosswise

12 large eggs

Salt and black pepper

1. Preheat the oven to 400°F (200°C, or gas mark 6). Grease a 12-cup muffin tin with oil, making sure you cover both the sides and the bottom of each cup. Wipe up any excess oil so you don't have oil pooling in the bottom of the cups.

2. Crisscross 2 bacon halves in the bottom of each cup to create an *X*.

3. Bake for 10 to 12 minutes. If the bacon you're using is thick (you did buy the better bacon, didn't you?), bake for 12 minutes. If you're using a fairly thin bacon (typically what's available in most supermarkets), 10 minutes will be fine. Your bacon will not be quite done.

4. Remove from the oven and carefully crack an egg on top of the bacon in each cup. Sprinkle with salt and black pepper.

5. Place back in the oven for 10 minutes or until the egg whites are set and the egg yolks are cooked to how you like them. Serve immediately!

taco skillet breakfast hash

Hash is my go-to breakfast solution because you can throw anything into the skillet with diced potatoes and *voilà*! You made a hash! This one is especially fun because we also have peppers, onions, taco-seasoned ground turkey or beef, and homemade pico de gallo. Those are a lot of big flavors to start your day off right! Make it really special by topping it off with black olives, fresh cilantro, guacamole, and/or avocado slices.

PREP TIME 10 minutes
TOTAL TIME 30 minutes
MAKES 2 to 4 servings

BREAKFAST HASH & EGGS
2 tablespoons (28 ml) extra-virgin olive oil or (28 g) coconut oil

2 medium sweet potatoes, cut into ½-inch (1 cm) cubes

½ red bell pepper, diced into ½-inch (1 cm) pieces

½ green bell pepper, diced into ½-inch (1 cm) pieces

¼ yellow or white onion, diced into ½-inch (1 cm) pieces

½ teaspoon salt, divided, plus more to taste

¼ teaspoon black pepper, plus more to taste

½ pound (225 g) ground turkey or beef

½ teaspoon chili powder

¼ teaspoon garlic powder

¼ teaspoon onion powder

¼ teaspoon dried oregano

⅛ teaspoon paprika

4 large eggs

PICO DE GALLO
1 medium tomato, diced into ½-inch (1 cm) or smaller pieces

½ large onion, diced into ½-inch (1 cm) or smaller pieces

Handful of cilantro, chopped

Fresh lime juice, to taste

Salt, to taste

¼ to ½ small jalapeño, seeded and diced (optional)

1. Make the Breakfast Hash & Eggs: Add the oil to a large skillet over medium-high heat. Once hot, add the potatoes, bell peppers, and onion. Sauté, stirring occasionally, until the potatoes have browned, about 5 minutes. Stir in ¼ teaspoon of the salt and the black pepper. Remove from the skillet and set aside.

2. Add the ground meat to the skillet and return to medium-high heat. Crumble the meat using your spatula and sauté until browned and cooked through, about 7 minutes. Stir in the chili powder, garlic powder, onion powder, oregano, remaining ¼ teaspoon salt, and paprika.

3. Meanwhile, make the Pico de Gallo: In a small bowl, combine the tomato, onion, cilantro, lime juice, and salt. Stir and set aside.

4. Add the cooked potato mixture back to the skillet with the ground meat, stirring to combine.

5. Use your spatula to create four holes in the hash. Crack one egg into each hole and sprinkle with salt and black pepper. Cover the skillet and reduce the heat to medium. Cook until the egg whites are set and the egg yolks are cooked to how you like them, 5 to 8 minutes.

6. Top everything with your homemade Pico de Gallo. Garnish as desired.

muffuletta egg scramble

All those flavors we associate with a classic muffuletta sandwich can now be enjoyed for breakfast in this tasty egg scramble. Roasted red peppers, salami, olives, and parsley … this is definitely not your typical breakfast fare!

PREP TIME 10 minutes
TOTAL TIME 20 minutes
MAKES 4 servings

¼ cup (45 g) chopped
roasted red peppers, drained

¼ cup (35 g) chopped
salami or pepperoni

2 tablespoons (18 g) sliced
kalamata or black olives

2 tablespoons (13 g) chopped
pimento-stuffed green olives

1 tablespoon (4 g) chopped
fresh parsley

1 teaspoon red wine vinegar

½ teaspoon minced garlic

8 large eggs

1 tablespoon (6 g) Italian
seasoning

½ teaspoon salt

½ teaspoon black pepper

2 tablespoons (28 g) ghee
(see Tip)

1. In a small bowl, stir together the roasted red peppers, salami or pepperoni, olives, parsley, vinegar, and garlic. Set aside.

2. In a medium bowl, whisk together the eggs, ¼ cup (60 ml) water (this helps make them fluffy), Italian seasoning, salt, and black pepper.

3. Add the ghee to a large skillet over medium heat. Once hot, pour in the eggs and the olive mixture. Use a spatula to fold the cooked outer edges of the eggs toward the center. Do this repeatedly until you don't have any more liquid in the skillet.

TIP
• You can easily substitute a different cooking fat for ghee if you're completely dairy free or just prefer the alternative.

sheet-pan breakfast fries

Who says fries aren't appropriate breakfast food? Don't listen to them. We don't need that kind of negativity in our lives. These breakfast fries are fun with baked eggs, diced turkey bacon, and an easy sauce! You'll definitely need a fork for these tender and loaded fries!

PREP TIME 10 minutes
TOTAL TIME 30 minutes
MAKES 3 servings

BREAKFAST FRIES & EGGS
3 medium sweet potatoes, sliced into sticks ¼ to ½ inch (6 mm to 1 cm) wide

3 tablespoons (45 ml) extra-virgin olive oil

½ teaspoon garlic powder

½ teaspoon paprika

½ teaspoon salt, plus more to taste

¼ teaspoon chili powder

6 slices turkey bacon, diced

6 large eggs

Black pepper, to taste

COMEBACK SAUCE
½ cup (115 g) high-quality mayo

1 tablespoon (15 g) ketchup

1 teaspoon fresh lemon juice

½ teaspoon Tabasco sauce or similar Louisiana-style hot sauce

½ teaspoon paprika

½ teaspoon garlic powder

½ teaspoon ground mustard

½ teaspoon salt

1. Make the Breakfast Fries & Eggs: Preheat the oven to 425°F (220°C, or gas mark 7). Line a 12 x 17-inch (30 x 43 cm) baking sheet with parchment paper.

2. Toss the sweet potatoes with the oil, garlic powder, paprika, salt, and chili powder on the prepared baking sheet. Spread in an even layer.

3. Scatter the bacon on the baking sheet with the fries.

4. Bake for 12 minutes.

5. Remove from the oven and create six spaces for your eggs. (Position the fries so that they will prevent the egg whites from running.) Crack one egg into each space. Sprinkle with salt and black pepper. Bake until the egg whites are set and the egg yolks are cooked to how you like them, 6 to 10 minutes.

6. Meanwhile, make the Comeback Sauce: In a small bowl, stir together the mayo, ketchup, lemon juice, Tabasco sauce, paprika, garlic powder, mustard, and salt.

7. When the fries are done, drizzle the sauce on top. Now, break out the forks!

TIP
- Check the ingredients on your mayo, ketchup, and Louisiana-style hot sauce. There are some really tasty brands available that are made with simple ingredients and no sugar.

- Comeback Sauce is a mayonnaise-based dipping sauce that originated in Jackson, Mississippi, and is thought to have its origins from Greek immigrants who settled in that area in the 1930's.

one-pan country breakfast

When you order a country breakfast in a restaurant, you'll usually receive a plate of cheesy eggs, potatoes with bell peppers, and ham or bacon. My spin on it is better for you but still ridiculously tasty. We're keeping it low carb with butternut squash, and it's dairy free, of course.

PREP TIME 5 minutes
TOTAL TIME 15 minutes
MAKES 4 serving

2 tablespoons (28 ml) extra-virgin olive oil, divided

1 red bell pepper, diced into ½-inch (1 cm) pieces

½ white or yellow onion, diced into ½-inch (1 cm) pieces

1 cup (140 g) diced butternut squash, ¾ to 1 inch (2 to 2.5 cm) cubes (see Tip)

1 cup chopped cooked (140 g) turkey, (150 g) ham, or (140 g) chicken

8 large eggs

½ teaspoon salt

¼ teaspoon black pepper

1. Add 1 tablespoon (15 ml) of the olive oil to a large skillet over medium-high heat. Once hot, add the bell pepper and onion. Sauté, stirring occasionally, for 2 minutes. (They won't be quite finished yet.) Add the squash and cooked protein. Sauté everything until the squash is tender, the onion is softened, and the bell pepper has some browning, 3 to 5 minutes.

2. Meanwhile, in a medium bowl, whisk together the eggs, ¼ cup (60 ml) water, salt, and black pepper. Set aside.

3. Reduce the heat to medium or medium-low. Add the remaining 1 tablespoon (15 ml) oil to the skillet. Pour the eggs over the squash mixture. Use a spatula to fold the cooked outer edges of the eggs toward the center. Do this repeatedly until you don't have any more liquid in the pan.

TIP

- Cut the butternut squash into cubes ¾ to 1 inch (2 to 2.5 cm) big. Some grocery stores carry prechopped squash in this very size. It's a huge time-saver!

- This is a great recipe for using leftover Thanksgiving turkey, rotisserie chicken, or holiday ham. Deli meat works well here, too.

skillet egg & veggie scramble

Are you tired of boring eggs? Well, this scramble will change your mind! Salsa and sautéed veggies make these eggs next-level good. You'll never want to make plain scrambled eggs again.

PREP TIME 5 minutes
TOTAL TIME 15 minutes
MAKES 4 servings

2 tablespoons (28 g)
ghee, divided

1 cup (71 g) chopped
broccoli florets

½ white or yellow onion, diced
into ½-inch (1 cm) pieces

8 large eggs

¼ cup (65 g) salsa

½ teaspoon salt

¼ teaspoon black pepper

1 packed cup (about half
a 5-ounce, or 140 g,
package) baby spinach

½ cup (90 g) halved
grape tomatoes

1. Add 1 tablespoon (14 g) of the ghee to a large skillet over medium-high heat. Once hot, add the broccoli and onion. Sauté, stirring occasionally, until the onion is tender and you see some browning on the broccoli, 3 to 5 minutes.

2. Meanwhile, whisk together the eggs, salsa, salt, and black pepper in a bowl. Set aside.

3. When the onions and broccoli are done, reduce the heat to medium or medium-low. Add the remaining 1 tablespoon (14 g) ghee to the skillet. Pour in the egg mixture, spinach, and tomatoes. Use a spatula to fold the cooked outer edges of the eggs toward the center. Do this repeatedly until you don't have any more liquid in the skillet.

salsa chicken egg muffins

These savory muffins are perfect for meal prep or for when you want a healthy breakfast option for a crowd. Serve them with extra salsa or even guacamole. Or, keep them stocked in the fridge for a grab-and-go breakfast!

PREP TIME 10 minutes
TOTAL TIME 20 minutes
MAKES 12 muffins

1½ tablespoons (25 ml) extra-virgin olive oil

12 large eggs

½ cup (130 g) salsa

½ teaspoon salt

½ teaspoon black pepper

¼ cup (8 g) chopped fresh spinach

¾ cup (94 g) shredded cooked chicken (see Tip)

Fresh jalapeño slices (optional)

1. Preheat the oven to 350°F (180°C, or gas mark 4). Grease a 12-cup muffin tin with the oil. Don't skimp on this or your eggs will stick. Make sure you grease both the sides and the bottom of each muffin cup.

2. In a large bowl, whisk together the eggs with the salsa, salt, and black pepper.

3. Pour the egg mixture evenly into each cup, so they're about three-fourths of the way full (or a little more).

4. Divide the spinach among each cup and use a fork to push the spinach down a bit. Divide the chicken among the cups. Add a slice of jalapeño to the top of your muffins, if using. (I do this for half of my egg muffins so that I have six that are spicy and six that aren't.)

5. Bake until the eggs are puffed and just set, about 20 minutes. Remove from the oven and set aside to cool. The egg muffins will puff up a lot while baking but will settle down over the next 5 minutes as they cool. Once cooled, use a fork or small spatula to gently pull the egg muffins from the pan.

TIP

- Purchase a rotisserie chicken from your grocery store to save time.

- Try these optional additions: diced onion, diced bell pepper, or fresh cilantro.

- To reheat muffins, microwave each for around 15 seconds, adding more time, if necessary.

- To freeze, pop completely cooled muffins into a resealable plastic bag and place them in the freezer. When you're ready to reheat, wrap each muffin in a wet paper towel (to help hold in the moisture) and heat in the microwave for about 30 seconds, adding more time, if necessary.

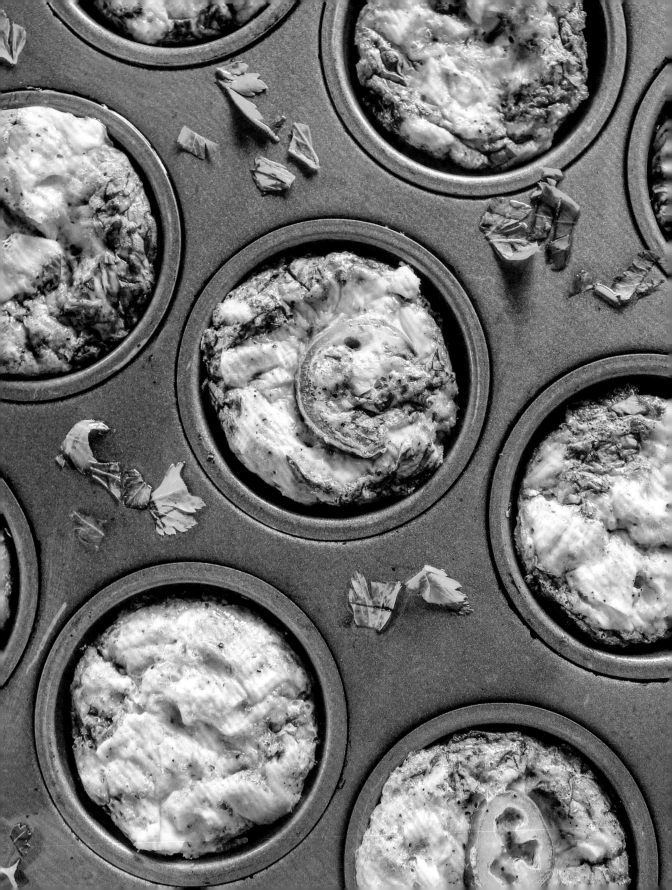

skillet sausage sweet potato hash

This simple hash has plenty of flavor and comes together in 25 minutes!

PREP TIME 10 minutes
TOTAL TIME 25 minutes
MAKES 4 servings

2 tablespoons (28 ml) extra-virgin olive oil or cooking fat of choice

2 cups (266 g) diced sweet potatoes, ½-inch (1 cm) cubes

¼ white or yellow onion, diced into ½-inch (1 cm) pieces

1 teaspoon salt, divided, plus more to taste

¼ teaspoon paprika

½ pound (225 g) ground turkey or pork sausage

½ teaspoon chili powder

½ teaspoon dried oregano

¼ teaspoon garlic powder

¼ teaspoon black pepper, plus more to taste

4 large eggs

1. Add the oil to a large skillet over medium-high heat. Once hot, add the potatoes and onion. Sauté, stirring occasionally, until the potatoes have browned and the onion is tender, about 5 minutes. Stir in ½ teaspoon of the salt and the paprika. Remove from the skillet and set aside.

2. Crumble the ground meat into the skillet and return to medium-high heat. Sauté until browned and cooked through, about 7 minutes. Stir in the remaining ½ teaspoon salt, chili powder, oregano, garlic powder, and black pepper.

3. Add the potatoes and onions back to the skillet. Use your spatula to create four holes in the hash. Crack one egg into each hole and sprinkle with salt and pepper. Cover the skillet and reduce the heat to medium. Cook until the egg whites are set and the yolks are cooked to how you like them, 5 to 8 minutes.

farmer's frittata

Frittatas are one of my favorite ways to celebrate breakfast because there are so many ways to mix up the flavors! Plus, they always look extra special so guests think you've been working hard in the kitchen. There's no need to tell them how easy this frittata is to throw together. It will be our secret.

PREP TIME 10 minutes
TOTAL TIME 30 minutes
MAKES 8 slices

1 cup (133 g) diced sweet potatoes, ½-inch (1 cm) cubes

5 slices bacon (turkey or pork), diced

¼ white or yellow onion, diced into ½-inch (1 cm) pieces

9 large eggs

1 teaspoon salt

½ teaspoon black pepper

¼ teaspoon ground mustard

½ cup (75 g) cherry or (90 g) grape tomatoes, halved

2 scallions, thinly sliced

2 tablespoons (8 g) chopped fresh parsley

1. Preheat the oven to 425°F (220°C, or gas mark 7).

2. Add the sweet potatoes, bacon, and onion to a large cast-iron skillet over medium-high heat. Sauté until the veggies are softened, about 5 minutes. (If using turkey bacon, add 2 tablespoons [28 ml] cooking fat to the skillet.)

3. Meanwhile, in a large bowl, whisk together the eggs, ½ cup (120 ml) water, salt, black pepper, and mustard.

4. Turn off the stove. Spread the sweet potato mixture across the bottom of the skillet so it's evenly distributed. Pour in the egg mixture. Sprinkle the tomatoes, scallions, and parsley on top.

5. Bake until just set, 10 to 12 minutes. Check to make sure the center isn't wiggly and then remove from the oven. Let your frittata rest for 5 minutes before serving.

TIP

- Cast iron is a naturally nonstick surface, so if it's been seasoned correctly, food won't stick. However, if your cast iron isn't well cared for, then sticking may be an issue. If you're concerned about the state of your skillet, wipe it down with olive oil before using it for this frittata recipe. After each use, wipe the inside of your skillet with a very thin layer of olive oil, just enough that the skillet is glossy. You don't want any oil to pool and settle when you put the skillet away or it will get sticky. You'll soon start to love your cast-iron skillet again!

bacon, egg, & sweet potato skillet

If you don't have any experience making a hash, this is the perfect recipe to start with! And who doesn't enjoy bacon, eggs, and potatoes? This uncomplicated breakfast skillet wins everybody over and is ready in about 15 minutes.

PREP TIME 5 minutes
TOTAL TIME 15 minutes
MAKES 4 servings

2 tablespoons (28 ml) extra-virgin olive oil or cooking fat of choice

4 cups (532 g) diced sweet potatoes, ½-inch (1 cm) cubes

4 slices bacon (turkey or pork), chopped (see Tip)

½ teaspoon salt, plus more to taste

½ teaspoon black pepper, plus more to taste

½ teaspoon paprika

4 large eggs

3 scallions, sliced

1. Add the oil to a large skillet over medium-high heat. Once hot, add the potatoes and bacon. Sauté, stirring occasionally, until the potatoes have browned, about 5 minutes. The potatoes won't be completely cooked through at this point. We just want them to have some color and crispy edges. Add the salt, black pepper, and paprika, stirring to combine.

2. Use your spatula to create four holes in the hash. Crack one egg into each hole. Sprinkle with salt and black pepper. Cover the skillet and reduce the heat to medium. Cook until the egg whites are set and the egg yolks are cooked to how you like them, 5 to 8 minutes. Sprinkle with the scallions before serving.

TIP
• We're using chopped bacon here (not crumbled) so it's substantial enough to hold up to the sweet potatoes but also small enough to cook quickly.

enchilada breakfast casserole

Think enchiladas should be eaten all day for all the meals? Well, I sure do! This breakfast casserole actually includes chicken enchiladas and is topped with an easy green enchilada sauce, cilantro, avocado, and tomatoes. Oh my!

PREP TIME 10 minutes
TOTAL TIME 30 minutes
MAKES 8 servings

ENCHILADA BREAKFAST CASSEROLE

1 tablespoon (15 ml) extra-virgin olive oil

1¾ cups (455 g) salsa, divided

3 cups (375 g) shredded cooked chicken

8 grain-free tortillas

12 large eggs

1½ teaspoons salt

½ teaspoon black pepper

¼ teaspoon ground cumin

¼ cup (4 g) chopped cilantro

1 avocado, sliced

1 cup (80 g) grape or (75 g) cherry tomatoes, halved

GREEN ENCHILADA SAUCE

2 cans (4 ounces, or 115 g, each) diced green chiles

1 medium jalapeño pepper, seeded

2 teaspoons minced garlic

½ teaspoon salt, plus more to taste

½ teaspoon ground cumin

1. Make the Enchilada Breakfast Casserole: Preheat the oven to 450°F (230°C, or gas mark 8). Grease the bottom and sides of 9 x 13-inch (23 x 33 cm) baking dish with the oil. Spread ½ cup (130 g) of the salsa on the bottom.

2. In a large bowl, combine 1 cup (260 g) of the salsa and all the shredded chicken.

3. Lay a tortilla on a clean surface. Add a small scoop (a little more than ¼ cup [35 g]) of the chicken mixture down the center of the tortilla. Carefully roll it up (be gentle because grain-free tortillas can be fragile) and place it seam-side down in the baking dish. Repeat with all the tortillas until you have 8 filled tortillas in your dish. (If you have any remaining salsa/chicken mixture, just add it in the empty spaces in your baking dish.)

4. In a separate large bowl, whisk together the eggs, remaining ¼ cup (65 g) salsa, salt, black pepper, and cumin. Pour over the rolled tortillas.

5. Bake until the eggs are puffed and just set, 18 to 20 minutes. Check to make sure the center isn't wiggling.

6. Meanwhile, make the Green Enchilada Sauce: To your high-powered blender or food processor, add the chiles (with their liquid), ½ cup (120 ml) water, jalapeño, garlic, salt, and cumin. Purée until smooth.

7. When the casserole is done, pour half of the sauce over top. Add the cilantro, avocado, and tomatoes. Add the remaining sauce to the casserole as you plate it.

4

sheet-pan & baking-dish dinners

There's just something so satisfying about tossing everything on a sheet pan (or in a baking dish) and letting it all roast until it's time to eat. It almost feels like cheating, doesn't it? Surely, dinner should be harder than this? But no, my friend. No need to complicate things. Let's keep it simple!

In this chapter, I'm sharing some of my favorite sheet-pan meals with you, and I just know you're going to love them as much as I do. Some of these recipes have marinating (always oh so worth it) or rest time, but it's hands-off time. Use that rest time to set the table, do a quick cleanup, or put your feet up!

Each recipe will require either a sheet pan (also known as a baking sheet) or a baking dish. Throughout this chapter, I will specify the size sheet pan or baking dish I use for the recipe. As a general rule, if you want to prepare a full sheet-pan meal (meaning an entree and at least one side), you'll want to use a sheet pan or baking sheet that is at least 12 x 17

inches (30 x 43 cm). Every recipe has been tested at that size to make sure everything fits. You may always use a larger sheet pan if you have one. You can also use two quarter-sheet pans, measuring 9½ x 13 inches (24 x 33 cm), if you prefer. If I recommend using parchment paper, I will say so. Otherwise, you can assume that I prepare that meal without any.

For recipes that call for a baking dish, I recommend one that is 9 x 13 inches (23 x 33 cm) and either glass or ceramic. I personally use and test all baking-dish recipes using ceramic.

easy cashew chicken

Serve up this easy chicken dish on any busy weeknight! Chicken, cashews, broccoli, red bell pepper, and the tastiest 4-ingredient sauce ever—what's not to love? It has all the flavor you want in exceptional takeout, but it's better for you. Feel free to swap out the chicken for pork tenderloin, if that's what you have on hand.

PREP TIME 10 minutes
TOTAL TIME 25 minutes
MAKES 4 servings

4-INGREDIENT SAUCE
½ cup (120 ml)
coconut aminos

1 tablespoon (15 ml) rice
or apple cider vinegar

1 tablespoon (10 g)
minced garlic

¼ to ½ teaspoon crushed
red pepper flakes

CASHEW CHICKEN & VEGGIES
1½ pounds (680 g) boneless,
skinless chicken breast, cut
into 1-inch (2.5 cm) pieces

12 ounces (340 g) broccoli
florets, large florets cut in
half or thirds

1 red bell pepper,
sliced into strips

Salt and black pepper
to taste

2 tablespoons (28 ml)
extra-virgin olive oil

¾ cup (105 g) roasted
cashews, salted or unsalted

1. Preheat the oven to 425°F (220°C, or gas mark 7).

2. Make the 4-Ingredient Sauce: In a bowl, whisk together the coconut aminos, vinegar, garlic, and red pepper flakes (use more for spicier flavor!). Set aside.

3. Make the Cashew Chickenn & Veggies: Spread the chicken in a single layer on one side of a 12 x 17-inch (30 x 43 cm) baking sheet.

4. Add the broccoli in a single layer beside your chicken.

5. Spread the bell pepper in a single layer beside the broccoli.

6. Sprinkle salt and black pepper over everything. Drizzle the oil over the broccoli and bell pepper. Drizzle half the sauce over the chicken. (Save the other half for later.) Bake for 10 minutes.

7. Remove from the oven and separate the chicken if it's sticking together. Make room for the cashews and add directly to the pan. Bake for 5 additional minutes.

8. Remove from the oven and make sure your chicken is cooked through, completely opaque and juices run clear. Layer the broccoli, bell pepper, chicken, and cashews in bowls or on plates. Drizzle the remaining sauce on top just before serving.

TIP
- In most recipes, I mention using parchment paper on your baking sheet. I don't use any for this particular recipe, but you're welcome to if you'd like to further minimize cleanup.

- I love to serve this recipe over steamed cauliflower rice to create larger portion sizes and add an extra boost of veggies!

arroz con pollo

This fun and light twist on a classic Spanish chicken dish is so flavorful you are going to want to make it again and again. Juicy chicken thighs coated in a homemade adobo seasoning bake with veggie-packed cauliflower rice for a bold sheet-pan meal.

PREP TIME 8 minutes

TOTAL TIME 30 minutes + rest time

MAKES 4 servings

ADOBO SEASONING

1½ teaspoons salt

1 teaspoon paprika

½ teaspoon dried oregano

½ teaspoon black pepper

¼ teaspoon chili powder

¼ teaspoon ground cumin

¼ teaspoon onion powder

¼ teaspoon garlic powder

CHICKEN

1½ to 2 pounds (680 to 900 g) boneless, skinless chicken thighs

1 tablespoon (15 ml) extra-virgin olive oil

CAULIFLOWER RICE

3 cups (12 ounces, or 340 g) cauliflower rice

1 cup (180 g) halved grape tomatoes

½ green bell pepper, diced into ½-inch (1 cm) pieces

½ red bell pepper, diced into ½-inch (1 cm) pieces

½ white or yellow onion, diced into ½-inch (1 cm) pieces

1 tablespoon (15 ml) extra-virgin olive oil

Small handful of fresh parsley, chopped

1. Preheat the oven to 425°F (220°C, or gas mark 7).

2. Make the Adobo Seasoning: In a small bowl, combine the salt, paprika, oregano, black pepper, chili powder, cumin, onion powder, and garlic powder. Set aside.

3. Make the Chicken: Pat the chicken thighs dry. Rub the oil on the chicken, focusing most of it on the top. Press all but 1 teaspoon of the Adobo Seasoning onto the top of your chicken. Place the chicken on one side of a 12 x 17-inch (30 x 43 cm) sheet pan.

4. Make the Cauliflower Rice: Spread the cauliflower rice on the empty side of your sheet pan. Add the tomatoes, bell peppers, and onion to the cauliflower. Drizzle the oil over the veggies and sprinkle on another 1 teaspoon Adobo Seasoning.

5. Bake for 20 minutes. This cooks fairly quickly since we're using boneless thighs. To crisp the top of the chicken a bit, broil on high for 2 to 3 minutes after the baking time finishes.

6. Remove from the oven and cover the sheet pan with aluminum foil. Let the chicken rest for 10 minutes so that it's tender and completely cooked through to a minimum internal temperature of 165°F (74°C). Top the Cauliflower Rice with the parsley before serving.

lemon-garlic mahi mahi with carrots

A quick and buttery lemon-garlic sauce transforms this fish into something truly spectacular. Pair with tender carrots (one of my favorite veggies to roast because of their natural sweetness), and you won't be disappointed!

PREP TIME 5 minutes
TOTAL TIME 30 minutes
MAKES 4 servings

1 pound (455 g) carrots, peeled and cut into sticks

4 tablespoons (56 g) ghee, melted,
or (60 ml) extra-virgin olive oil, divided

¾ teaspoon salt, divided

4 mahi mahi fillets (see Tip) (6 to 8 ounces, or 170 to 225 g, each)

1½ tablespoons (25 ml) fresh lemon juice

1 tablespoon (10 g) minced garlic

1 tablespoon (4 g) chopped fresh parsley

1. Preheat the oven to 425°F (220°C, or gas mark 7).

2. Spread the carrots in one half of a 9 x 13-inch (23 x 33 cm) baking dish. Top with 2 tablespoons (28 g) of the ghee and ¼ teaspoon of the salt. Bake for 15 minutes.

3. Remove from the oven and reduce the temperature to 375°F (190°C, or gas mark 5).

4. Add the mahi mahi beside the carrots. Top the fish with the remaining 2 tablespoons (28 g) ghee, remaining ½ teaspoon salt, lemon juice, and garlic. Bake until the fish is opaque and flakes easily with a fork, 9 to 10 minutes.

5. To serve, divide the carrots among plates, along with a piece of fish. Sprinkle the fresh parsley over the mahi mahi.

TIP
- You can easily swap out the mahi mahi for another fish if you like. Tilapia or flounder would work well!

sheet-pan mini meatloaves & sweet potatoes

This Paleo spin on a classic comfort food is so easy but tastes just like you remember from childhood. There are no breadcrumbs to be found—and you won't miss them!

PREP TIME 10 minutes
TOTAL TIME 30 minutes
MAKES 4 servings

MINI MEATLOAVES
1½ pounds (680 g) 93% lean ground beef

½ cup (80 g) finely diced white or yellow onion

⅓ cup (37 g) almond flour

3 tablespoons (45 g) plus ⅓ cup (80 g) ketchup, divided (see Tip)

2 large eggs

1½ tablespoons (15 g) minced garlic

1 teaspoon salt

¾ teaspoon dried thyme

¾ teaspoon dried parsley

¾ teaspoon onion powder

½ teaspoon black pepper

SWEET POTATOES
2 or 3 medium sweet potatoes, cut into 1-inch (2.5 cm) cubes

2 tablespoons (28 ml) extra-virgin olive oil

1 teaspoon salt

1 teaspoon garlic powder

½ teaspoon paprika

1. Make the Mini Meatloaves: Preheat the oven to 450°F (230°C, or gas mark 8). Line a 12 x 17-inch (30 x 43 cm) baking sheet with parchment paper.

2. In a large bowl, combine the ground beef, onion, almond flour, 3 tablespoons (45 g) ketchup, eggs, garlic, salt, thyme, parsley, onion powder, and black pepper. Use your hands or a spatula to mix everything together until well combined.

3. Use your hands to form eight mini loaves of the same size. Place them so they're not touching on half of the prepared baking sheet.

4. Make the Sweet Potatoes: In a medium bowl, toss the sweet potatoes in the oil, salt, garlic powder, and paprika to evenly coat. Spread in a single layer beside the mini meatloaves.

5. Bake for 15 minutes.

6. Remove from the oven. Spread the remaining ⅓ cup (80 g) ketchup across the tops of your mini meatloaves. Bake until the mini meatloaves are cooked through to a minimum internal temperature of 165°F (74°C) and the sweet potatoes are tender, about 5 more minutes.

TIP
- Check the ingredients on the ketchup label. There are several fantastic options sweetened without sugar or corn syrup, but take a minute to peruse your options in the grocery store. You may find that the ketchup you've been purchasing for years contains a lot of unappealing junk.

barbecue chicken thighs with spicy broccoli

I love using chicken thighs rather than chicken breasts when possible because they are close to impossible to overcook and stay so juicy! You will appreciate how tender these are. Slather them with a surprisingly easy homemade and sugar-free barbecue sauce for the perfect entree paired with crispy broccoli.

PREP TIME 8 minutes
TOTAL TIME 30 minutes
+ rest time
MAKES 4 servings

CHICKEN THIGHS & SPICY BROCCOLI

1½ to 1¾ pounds (680 to 795 g) boneless, skinless chicken thighs

3 tablespoons (45 ml) extra-virgin olive oil, divided

½ teaspoon salt, plus more to taste

Black pepper, to taste

12 ounces (340 g) broccoli florets

¼ teaspoon garlic powder

¼ teaspoon crushed red pepper flakes

BARBECUE SAUCE

1 cup (240 g) ketchup

½ cup (120 ml) coconut aminos

2 teaspoons chili powder

1½ teaspoons ground mustard

1 teaspoon apple cider vinegar

1 teaspoon minced garlic

1 teaspoon salt

¼ teaspoon garlic powder

1. Make the Chicken Thighs with Spicy Broccoli: Preheat the oven to 425°F (220°C, or gas mark 7).

2. Pat the chicken thighs dry. Rub 1 tablespoon (15 ml) of the oil on the chicken, focusing most of it on the top. Place the chicken on one side of a 12 x 17-inch (30 x 43 cm) sheet pan. Sprinkle with salt and black pepper.

3. Spread the broccoli in an even layer beside the chicken. Drizzle with the remaining 2 tablespoons (28 ml) oil. Sprinkle with the ½ teaspoon salt, garlic powder, and red pepper flakes.

4. Bake for 10 minutes.

5. Meanwhile, make the Barbecue Sauce: In a medium bowl, combine the ketchup, coconut aminos, chili powder, mustard, vinegar, garlic, salt, and garlic powder. Divide between two bowls and set aside.

6. Remove the chicken and broccoli from the oven and brush the chicken with half of the sauce. Reserve the remaining sauce for later.

7. Bake for another 10 minutes. To crisp the top of the chicken a bit, broil for 2 to 3 minutes after the baking time finishes.

8. Remove from the oven. Brush the remaining half of the sauce on top of the chicken. Cover the sheet pan with aluminum foil. Let the chicken rest for 10 minutes so that it's tender and completely cooked through to a minimum internal temperature of 165°F (74°C).

sheet-pan sausage & veggies

This is the meal I turn to on those busy weeknights when I'm just barely holding on until bedtime. It just doesn't get much easier than this. Chop. Drizzle. Sprinkle. Bake. BOOM. Dinner is served.

PREP TIME 10 minutes
TOTAL TIME 30 minutes
MAKES 4 servings

1 pound (455 g) green beans, trimmed and halved

1 pound (455 g) Brussels sprouts, trimmed and halved

4 fully cooked chicken sausages, sliced ¼ inch (6 mm) thick

3 tablespoons (45 ml) extra-virgin olive oil

Salt and black pepper to taste

1 tablespoon (10 g) minced garlic

1. Preheat the oven to 425°F (220°C, or gas mark 7).

2. Spread the green beans, Brussels sprouts, and sausage on a 12 x 17-inch (30 x 43 cm) baking sheet in a single layer.

3. Drizzle the oil over everything and sprinkle with salt and black pepper. Stir everything together so the oil is evenly distributed and then spread in a single layer.

4. Bake for 15 minutes.

5. Remove from the oven and add the garlic. Bake until the vegetables are tender with some crispy edges, another 5 to 10 minutes.

TIP
• Any fully cooked sausage will work well here, so feel free to use your favorite brand or go with turkey or beef.

• Green beans or Brussels sprouts can be swapped out for another veggie with a similar cooking time. Carrot sticks or diced potatoes (if diced fairly small) would be delicious!

baked fish & root vegetables

Roasting root vegetables caramelizes the natural sugar in them to bring out their sweetness. Combine that with a flaky white fish, here we are using cod, and you have one incredible meal!

PREP TIME 10 minutes
TOTAL TIME 30 minutes
MAKES 4 servings

ROOT VEGETABLES
2 cups (244 g) peeled, sliced carrots, ¼-inch (6 mm)-thick slices
2 cups (266 g) diced sweet potatoes, ½-inch (1 cm) cubes
1 red onion, sliced into large chunks
¼ cup (60 ml) extra-virgin olive oil
1 teaspoon salt
½ teaspoon black pepper

FISH
1½ tablespoons (25 ml) fresh lemon juice
1 tablespoon (4 g) finely chopped fresh parsley
1 teaspoon extra-virgin olive oil
¼ teaspoon salt
¼ teaspoon garlic powder
4 cod fillets (6 ounces, or 170 g, each)

1. Make the Root Vegetables: Preheat the oven to 450°F (230°C, or gas mark 8). Line a 12 x 17-inch (30 x 43 cm) baking sheet with parchment paper.

2. Spread the carrots, sweet potatoes, and onion on the prepared baking sheet in a single layer.

3. Drizzle the oil over the veggies and sprinkle with the salt and black pepper. Stir it all together so everything is coated. Spread in a single layer and then bake for 10 minutes.

4. Meanwhile, make the Fish: Combine the lemon juice, parsley, oil, salt, and garlic powder in a small bowl. Set aside.

5. Remove the pan from the oven and reduce the temperature to 425°F (220°C, or gas mark 7). Use a spatula to stir the vegetables. Spread in an even layer and create four holes or spaces on the baking sheet for your fish. Add the cod to the pan. Drizzle your lemon juice mixture over the top of the cod.

6. Bake until the fish is opaque and flakes easily with a fork and the vegetables are tender, 10 to 15 minutes.

balsamic flank steak

This juicy flank steak swims in a delicious vinaigrette and cooks with broiled peppers, onion, and mushrooms. The secret to this perfect steak is in the incredible and simple marinade, broiling at high heat, letting it rest before serving, and thinly slicing the steak across the grain when it's time to serve. Garnish with fresh herbs for a gorgeous meal.

PREP TIME 10 minutes
+ marinating time
TOTAL TIME 22 minutes
+ rest time
MAKES 6 servings

5 tablespoons (75 ml) extra-virgin olive oil, divided

¼ cup (60 ml) balsamic vinegar

¼ cup (60 ml) coconut aminos

1 tablespoon (2 g) chopped fresh rosemary

1½ teaspoons salt

1 teaspoon black pepper

1 teaspoon garlic powder

½ teaspoon onion powder

½ teaspoon chili powder

1½ pounds (680 g) flank steak

8 ounces (225 g) cremini or baby bella mushrooms, sliced

3 bell peppers of any color, sliced into strips

1 red onion, sliced into strips

1. In a resealable plastic bag or bowl, combine 3 tablespoons (45 ml) of the oil, vinegar, coconut aminos, rosemary, salt, black pepper, garlic powder, onion powder, and chili powder. Add the flank steak, seal the bag, and toss to coat. Refrigerate for a minimum of 1 hour and up to 12 hours before cooking.

2. When ready to cook, move the oven rack to 5 to 6 inches (13 to 15 cm) from the broiler and set the broiler to high. Grease a 12 x 17-inch (30 x 43 cm) baking sheet with the remaining 2 tablespoons (28 ml) oil.

3. Place the steak on the prepared baking sheet, leaving any remaining marinade in the bag or bowl for now.

4. Spread the mushrooms, bell peppers, and onion around the steak in an even layer. Drizzle the remaining marinade over the vegetables.

5. Broil for 6 minutes.

6. Remove the pan from the oven and flip your flank steak. Broil for another 6 minutes for medium-rare.

7. Remove the pan from the oven. Cover with aluminum foil and let the steak rest for at least 10 minutes. This results in more tender meat.

8. Slice the meat thinly against the grain when ready to eat. Don't forget to serve with that pan sauce!

TIP
- If preparing a larger flank steak, adjust the cooking time. If your steak is between 1¾ and 2 pounds (795 and 900 g), I suggest a total broiling time of about 14 minutes.

almond-crusted chicken dinner

If you are new to breading chicken with almond flour, you are going to be so pleased with how these chicken cutlets turn out. Perfectly breaded and seasoned chicken with lemony asparagus deserves a place on your menu.

PREP TIME 10 minutes
TOTAL TIME 30 minutes
MAKES 4 servings

**ALMOND-CRUSTED
CHICKEN CUTLET**

**2 tablespoons (28 ml)
extra-virgin olive oil**

**1¼ cups (140 g) finely ground
almond flour**

¾ teaspoon chili powder

¾ teaspoon garlic powder

¾ teaspoon dried parsley

¾ teaspoon dried basil

¾ teaspoon salt

2 large eggs

**2 tablespoons (28 ml)
coconut aminos**

**1 to 1½ pounds (455 to
680 g) chicken breast
cutlets, thinly sliced**

ASPARAGUS

**1 bunch asparagus, trimmed
(thick stalk works best)**

**1 tablespoon (15 ml)
extra-virgin olive oil**

Juice from ½ lemon

¼ teaspoon salt

1. Make the Almond-Crusted Chicken Cutlet: Preheat the oven to 450°F (230°C, or gas mark 8). Grease a 12 x 17-inch (30 x 43 cm) baking sheet with the oil.

2. In a shallow dish, combine the almond flour, chili powder, garlic powder, parsley, basil, and salt. Mix well.

3. In separate bowl, whisk together the eggs and coconut aminos.

4. Dredge each chicken cutlet in the egg mixture and let the excess drip off. Then, dredge each cutlet in the breading mixture.

5. Place each breaded cutlet on one side of the prepared baking sheet, leaving room for the asparagus later. Bake for 12 minutes.

6. Remove the pan from the oven. Carefully flip each cutlet. Be gentle so the breading doesn't stick to the pan.

7. Make the Asparagus: Add the asparagus beside the chicken. Drizzle with the oil and lemon juice. Sprinkle with the salt. Bake until the chicken is cooked through to a minimum internal temperature of 165°F (74°C), about 8 minutes more. (If using boneless pork chops, cook to a minimum internal temperature of 145°F [63°C].)

TIP
- To bread your chicken, lay a cutlet on top of the breading ingredients and use your fingers to cover the top of the cutlet with breading and press it into the chicken. Breading will stick to the bottom of your cutlet while you do this.

- Feel free to swap out the chicken for boneless pork chops.

turkey meatballs in marinara over butternut squash noodles

I'm a meatball junkie, which means I really think I could eat meatballs every day without growing bored. There are just so many ways to serve them up! This delightful meatball dinner is a bit different than your typical spaghetti and meatballs. It feels and tastes fresh because we are using minimal sauce and pairing the meatballs with thick butternut squash noodles—and it's all done on a sheet pan!

PREP TIME 15 minutes
TOTAL TIME 30 minutes
MAKES 4 servings

TURKEY MEATBALLS
1 pound (455 g) 93% lean ground turkey

¼ cup (28 g) almond flour

¼ cup (40 g) white or yellow onion, diced into ¼-inch (6 mm) pieces

¼ cup (16 g) finely chopped fresh parsley, plus more for garnish (optional)

1 large egg

1 tablespoon (10 g) minced garlic

1 teaspoon salt

½ teaspoon black pepper

½ teaspoon onion powder

EASY MARINARA SAUCE
16 ounces (455 g) canned tomato sauce

½ teaspoon salt

½ teaspoon dried basil

½ teaspoon dried oregano

BUTTERNUT SQUASH NOODLES
6 cups (about 22 ounces, or 625 g) butternut squash noodles

3 tablespoons (45 ml) extra-virgin olive oil

½ teaspoon salt

Chopped fresh basil, for garnish (optional)

1. Make the Turkey Meatballs: Preheat the oven to 450°F (230°C, or gas mark 8). Line a 12 x 17-inch (30 x 43 cm) baking sheet with parchment paper.

2. In a large bowl, combine the turkey, almond flour, onion, parsley, egg, garlic, salt, black pepper, and onion powder. Use a small cookie scoop or tablespoon to shape the meatballs. We want to keep them small (1 tablespoon [15 g] in size, or about 1 inch [2.5 cm]) so they'll cook quickly. You should have 20 to 22 meatballs. Lay them in a single layer on the prepared baking sheet, leaving a little space in between each.

3. Bake for 5 minutes.

4. Meanwhile, make the Easy Marinara Sauce: In a medium bowl, stir together the tomato sauce, salt, basil, and oregano.

5. Remove the baking sheet from the oven. Use a spatula or tongs to gently move the meatballs to one side of the pan. Pour the Easy Marinara Sauce over the meatballs.

6. Make the Butternut Squash Noodles: Spread the noodles on the open half of the baking sheet. Drizzle with the oil and sprinkle with the salt.

7. Bake until the meatballs are cooked through to a minimum internal temperature of 165°F (74°C) and the Butternut Squash Noodles are tender with a bit of crunch, 10 to 15 minutes.

8. Use tongs to add the Butternut Squash Noodles to each plate. Top with the meatballs and sauce. Garnish with additional fresh chopped parsley, or basil, if you like.

roasted cranberry chicken & brussels sprouts

Tart fresh cranberries burst as you roast them and add so much flavor to this chicken. I love it paired with crispy roasted Brussels sprouts! Cubed pork tenderloin would also be divine here, so feel free to swap out the chicken, if you want to change things up.

PREP TIME 10 minutes
TOTAL TIME 30 minutes
MAKES 6 to 8 servings

2 pounds (900 g) Brussels sprouts, trimmed and halved (if large)

12 ounces (340 g) fresh cranberries

4 tablespoons (60 ml) extra-virgin olive oil, divided

2 tablespoons (28 ml) pure maple syrup

2 tablespoons (28 ml) coconut aminos

2 pounds (900 g) boneless, skinless chicken breasts, cut into 1-inch (2.5 cm) pieces

1 tablespoon (2 g) finely chopped fresh rosemary

1½ teaspoons salt

1. Preheat the oven to 425°F (220°C, or gas mark 7). Line a 12 x 17-inch (30 x 43 cm) baking sheet with parchment paper.

2. Spread the Brussels sprouts and cranberries in an even layer on the prepared baking sheet. Drizzle 2 tablespoons (28 ml) of the oil over everything. Bake for 5 minutes.

3. Meanwhile, add the remaining 2 tablespoons (28 ml) oil, maple syrup, and coconut aminos to a small bowl. Stir until combined.

4. Remove the pan from the oven and add the chicken, mixing it in with the Brussels sprouts and cranberries. It's a tight fit, but it will fit. Pour the syrup mixture over everything and sprinkle with the rosemary and salt. Use a spatula to move the Brussels sprouts, cranberries, and chicken around so it's all well coated. Spread in an even layer.

5. Bake until the chicken is cooked through, completely opaque and juices run clear, about 15 minutes.

sheet-pan chicken cabbage stir-fry

A stir-fry prepared on a sheet pan? Yes, please! This stir-fry is fully loaded with cabbage, broccoli, Brussels sprouts, onion, and chicken. Roasting the veggies gives you all those crispy edges you love. Top with sriracha sauce for extra heat, and I swear you'll think it tastes like a classic pad Thai!

PREP TIME 10 minutes
TOTAL TIME 30 minutes
MAKES 4 servings

4 cups (280 g) shredded cabbage

2 cups (142 g) chopped broccoli

2 cups (176 g) Brussels sprouts, halved or quartered

½ white or yellow onion, thinly sliced

1 pound (455 g) chicken breasts, sliced into 1-inch (2.5 cm) pieces

2 tablespoons (28 ml) extra-virgin olive oil

1½ teaspoons minced garlic

½ teaspoon salt

½ teaspoon ground ginger

¼ cup (25 g) chopped scallions

3 tablespoons (45 ml) coconut aminos

Sriracha or hot sauce, for topping

1. Preheat the oven to 425°F (220°C, or gas mark 7).

2. Spread the cabbage, broccoli, Brussels sprouts, and onion on a 12 x 17-inch (30 x 43 cm) sheet pan. Add the chicken on top of the vegetables.

3. Drizzle the oil over everything. Add the garlic. Sprinkle with the salt and ginger.

4. Bake until the chicken is cooked through, completely opaque and juices run clear, and the veggies are tender with some crispiness, 20 to 25 minutes.

5. After roasting, add the scallions and coconut aminos. Stir to combine. Drizzle the sriracha or hot sauce over everything before serving.

TIP
- Sliced pork tenderloin would make an excellent substitution for the chicken, if that's what you have.

beef tips with veggies

Prepare yourself for one of my all-time favorites. This recipe was inspired by my mother-in-law, who always makes delicious beef tips. I've given it a Paleo spin and turned it into a one-pan meal by incorporating green beans. Make this recipe once, and you'll be making it a hundred times because it's just that good.

PREP TIME 10 minutes
+ marinating time
TOTAL TIME 25 minutes
MAKES 4 to 6 servings

MARINADE
¼ cup (60 ml) coconut aminos

¼ red (60 ml) wine vinegar

2 tablespoons (28 ml) extra-virgin olive oil

1 tablespoon (10 g) minced garlic

1 tablespoon (6 g) Italian seasoning

1 teaspoon salt

½ teaspoon black pepper

BEEF TIPS & VEGGIES
1½ pounds (680 g) top sirloin, sliced into strips ½ inch (1 cm) thick and 2 inches (5 cm) long

12 ounces (340 g) green beans, trimmed

1 white or yellow onion, cut into strips

1 green bell pepper, cut into strips

2½ tablespoons (40 ml) extra-virgin olive oil

½ teaspoon salt

1. Make the Marinade: In a resealable plastic bag or bowl, combine the marinade ingredients.

2. Make the Beef Tips & Veggies: Add the sirloin to the marinade, seal the bag, and toss to coat. Refrigerate for a minimum of 1 hour and up to 12 hours before cooking.

3. Set the oven rack to the middle position and turn the broiler on high.

4. Spread the green beans, onion, and bell pepper in a single layer on a 12 x 17-inch (30 x 43 cm) baking sheet. Drizzle with the oil and sprinkle with the salt. Broil for 10 minutes.

5. Add the marinated steak to the pan with your vegetables. Stir so that everything is in an even layer. If you have any marinade left, pour that in too. Broil until the steak is done to your liking, 4 to 5 minutes.

pesto chicken & green beans

A pesto without Parmesan? Gasp! You won't even notice it's missing. This easy pesto is bright, lemony, and addictive. I use it about one hundred different ways. You're going to love it on baked chicken.

PREP TIME 5 minutes
TOTAL TIME 30 minutes
MAKES 4 servings

CHICKEN & GREEN BEANS
3 tablespoons (45 ml) extra-virgin olive oil, divided

1½ pounds (680 g) boneless, skinless chicken breasts

12 ounces (340 g) fresh green beans, trimmed

1 teaspoon salt, divided

½ teaspoon black pepper

½ teaspoon garlic powder

½ teaspoon dried basil

PISTACHIO LEMON PESTO
3 cups (72 g) packed fresh basil

¼ cup (31 g) shelled pistachios

3 tablespoons (45 ml) fresh lemon juice

½ teaspoon minced garlic

½ teaspoon salt

⅓ cup (80 ml) extra-virgin olive oil

1. Make the Chicken & Green Beans: Preheat the oven to 450°F (230°C, or gas mark 8). Grease the bottom of a 9 x 13-inch (23 x 33 cm) baking dish with 1 tablespoon (15 ml) of the oil.

2. Place the chicken breasts in a single layer on one side of your baking dish. Add the green beans beside the chicken.

3. In a small bowl, stir together ¾ teaspoon of the salt, black pepper, garlic powder, and dried basil.

4. Brush 1 tablespoon (15 ml) of the oil on the top and bottom of the chicken. Pat the spice mixture onto all sides of the chicken.

5. Drizzle the remaining 1 tablespoon (15 ml) oil over the green beans and sprinkle with the remaining ¼ teaspoon salt.

6. Bake until the thickest part of the breast reaches a minimum internal temperature of 165°F (74°C), about 20 minutes.

7. Meanwhile, make the Pistachio Lemon Pesto: Add the fresh basil, pistachios, lemon juice, garlic, and salt to a food processor or high-powered blender. Turn on the blender and slowly pour in your oil. Blend until the pistachios are no longer chunky and the sauce is smooth. For a thick pesto, ⅓ cup (80 ml) oil is perfect. You can use up to ½ cup (120 ml) oil, if you prefer a thinner consistency.

8. Remove the chicken and green beans from the oven. Loosely cover the baking dish with aluminum foil and let the chicken rest for 5 to 10 minutes.

9. Top each chicken breast with a generous dollop of Pistachio Lemon Pesto when serving.

chimichurri steak dinner

I personally don't think you can go wrong with steak drizzled in any sauce, but this chimichurri is just extra special. It's tangy and has a little heat. And I would be remiss if I failed to mention how incredible these Brussels sprouts are, my friend. The marinade from the steak makes its way to the veggies as everything cooks, and it is pure magic.

PREP TIME 10 minutes
TOTAL TIME 30 minutes
MAKES 8 servings

STEAK & BRUSSELS SPROUTS

2 tablespoons (28 ml) coconut aminos

3 tablespoons (45 ml) extra-virgin olive oil, divided

1½ teaspoons salt, divided

½ teaspoon chili powder

½ teaspoon black pepper

2 pounds (900 g) sirloin steak, cut into strips ½ inch (1 cm) thick and 3 to 4 inches (7.5 to 10 cm) long

2 pounds (900 g) Brussels sprouts, trimmed and halved (if large)

CHIMICHURRI SAUCE

½ cup (30 g) tightly packed fresh parsley

3 tablespoons (45 ml) red wine vinegar

2 tablespoons (8 g) chopped fresh oregano

2 tablespoons (20 g) minced garlic

1 teaspoon crushed red pepper flakes

¼ teaspoon salt

¼ cup (60 ml) extra-virgin olive oil

1. Make the Steak & Brussels Sprouts: Preheat the oven to 425°F (220°C, or gas mark 7).

2. In a large bowl, combine the coconut aminos, 1 tablespoon (15 ml) of the oil, ¾ teaspoon of the salt, chili powder, and black pepper. Add the steak and toss to coat with the marinade. Set aside.

3. Spread the Brussels sprouts on one side of a 12 x 17-inch (30 x 43 cm) baking sheet. Drizzle with the remaining 2 tablespoons (28 ml) oil and sprinkle with the remaining ¾ teaspoon salt. Bake for 10 minutes.

4. Remove the pan from the oven. Add the marinated steak beside the Brussels sprouts. Bake until the steak is cooked how you like it and the Brussels sprouts are tender, 8 to 10 minutes.

5. Meanwhile, make the Chimichurri Sauce: Add the parsley, vinegar, oregano, garlic, red pepper flakes, and salt to a food processor. Pulse until the herbs are finely chopped. Slowly pour in the oil while pulsing. Scrape down the sides of the food processor if needed.

6. To serve, divide the Brussels sprouts and steak among plates. Drizzle your Chimichurri Sauce over the steak.

orange chicken cauliflower rice bowls

Cauliflower rice bowls are such a fun way to load up on veggies without feeling like you are loading up on veggies! I enjoy playing around with different flavor combinations, and this one features roasted veggies and chicken in a sticky orange sauce. Don't skip the zest!

PREP TIME 10 minutes
TOTAL TIME 30 minutes
MAKES 4 servings

CHICKEN & VEGGIES
12 ounces (340 g) fresh green beans, trimmed and halved

3 tablespoons (45 ml) extra-virgin olive oil, divided

2 cups (8 ounces, or 225 g) cauliflower rice

1 yellow or orange bell pepper, sliced into strips

1½ pounds (680 g) boneless, skinless chicken breasts, cut into 1-inch (2.5 cm) pieces

½ teaspoon salt

½ teaspoon garlic powder

ORANGE SAUCE
3 tablespoons (45 ml) fresh orange juice

2½ tablespoons (50 g) raw honey

1 tablespoon (15 ml) coconut aminos

1 tablespoon (6 g) orange zest

1 tablespoon (9 g) arrowroot flour

1 tablespoon (15 ml) cold water

1. Make the Chicken & Veggies: Preheat the oven to 400°F (200°C, or gas mark 6).

2. Add the green beans to a 12 x 17-inch (30 x 43 cm) baking sheet in a single layer. Drizzle 1 tablespoon (15 ml) of the oil on top. Bake for 5 minutes.

3. Meanwhile, prepare your Orange Sauce: Combine the orange juice, honey, coconut aminos, and orange zest in a small bowl. In a small jar, shake together the arrowroot flour and water to create a slurry. Stir the slurry into the sauce. Set aside.

4. Remove the green beans from the oven. Use a spatula to carefully move them to one side of the pan. Spread the cauliflower rice beside it, then the bell peppers, and then the chicken.

5. Drizzle the remaining 2 tablespoons (28 ml) oil over the bell peppers and cauliflower rice. Sprinkle the salt over everything on the baking sheet. Add the garlic powder to the chicken and green beans.

6. Pour the Orange Sauce over the chicken only. Use a spatula to move the chicken around in the sauce so the chicken is coated.

7. Bake for 10 minutes. The sauce will get bubbly as it heats up in the oven. That's great!

8. Remove from the oven and separate the chicken if it's sticking together. Use a spatula to push the sauce to the chicken if it's running into the vegetables. Return to the oven and bake until the chicken is cooked through, completely opaque and juices run clear, about 5 additional minutes.

9. Remove from the oven. Layer your cauliflower rice, green beans, bell pepper, and chicken in bowls. Top with any sauce remaining in the pan.

easy italian sausage & peppers

This Italian-inspired meal includes the hard-to-beat flavor combo of sausage, onion, and bell peppers. Add in fresh basil and throw it over roasted cauliflower rice for a seriously spectacular dinner that will earn rave reviews in your home.

PREP TIME 10 minutes
TOTAL TIME 30 minutes
MAKES 4 servings

12 ounces (340 g) fully cooked chicken sausages, sliced ¼ inch (6 mm) thick

1 red bell pepper, sliced into thin strips

1 yellow or orange bell pepper, sliced into thin strips

1 white or yellow onion, sliced into thin strips

4 tablespoons (60 ml) extra-virgin olive oil, divided

½ teaspoon garlic powder

½ teaspoon dried oregano

½ teaspoon dried basil

¾ teaspoon salt, divided

½ teaspoon black pepper

3 cups (12 ounces, or 340 g) cauliflower rice

5 or 6 large basil leaves, chopped

1. Preheat the oven to 425°F (220°C, or gas mark 7).

2. Spread the chicken sausage, bell peppers, and onion on a 12 x 17-inch (30 x 43 cm) baking sheet. Drizzle with 3 tablespoons (45 ml) of the oil, garlic powder, oregano, dried basil, ½ teaspoon of the salt, and black pepper. Use a spoon or spatula to stir so everything is evenly coated and then gently push the mixture to one side so you have enough room for your cauliflower rice.

3. Spread the cauliflower rice on the other side. Add the remaining 1 tablespoon (15 ml) oil and remaining ¼ teaspoon salt on top of the cauliflower.

4. Bake until the peppers and onions are tender, about 20 minutes.

5. Garnish with the fresh basil after baking. To serve, layer the cauliflower rice in bowls and top with the sausage, bell peppers, and onion.

pistachio-herb crusted salmon with asparagus

Just wait until you try the crust on this salmon! Made from pistachios, basil, and lemon juice, it's thick, so it really clings to the top of your gorgeous fish as it roasts. I highly recommend this for even the pickiest seafood eater!

PREP TIME 10 minutes
TOTAL TIME 25 minutes
MAKES 4 servings

PISTACHIO-HERB
CRUSTED SALMON
4 wild-caught salmon fillets (6 ounces, or 170 g, each)

½ cup (12 g) fresh basil

⅓ cup (41 g) shelled pistachios

2 tablespoons (28 ml) extra-virgin olive oil

2 tablespoons (28 ml) fresh lemon juice

½ teaspoon salt

½ teaspoon black pepper

ASPARAGUS
1 bunch fresh asparagus, trimmed

1 tablespoon (15 ml) extra-virgin olive oil

Salt, to taste

1. Make the Pistachio-Herb Crusted Salmon: Preheat the oven to 425°F (220°C, or gas mark 7).

2. Place the salmon, skin-side down, on a nonstick baking sheet or on a 12 x 17-inch (30 x 43 cm) baking sheet lined with parchment paper.

3. To a food processor or high-powered blender, add the basil, pistachios, oil, lemon juice, salt, and black pepper. Blend until you don't have any large chunks of pistachio.

4. Spread the mixture over the top of each salmon fillet. You'll want to use every single bit. (It's really good!)

5. Bake for 5 minutes. Remove from the oven.

6. Make the Asparagus: Add the asparagus to the baking sheet beside your salmon. Drizzle with the oil and sprinkle with salt.

7. Bake until the salmon is cooked through, opaque and flakes easily with a fork, and the asparagus is slightly wilted but still crunchy, an additional 8 to 10 minutes.

steak fajitas

There are so many ways to enjoy this tender fajita steak with peppers and onions! I love to serve it over lettuce for a healthy fajita salad. There are also plenty of grain-free tortilla options you might enjoy if you prefer the more traditional route. Whatever you choose, this recipe is sure to be on repeat in your house!

PREP TIME 10 minutes
TOTAL TIME 17 minutes
MAKES 4 servings

STEAK & VEGETABLES
1 pound (455 g) sirloin steak, cut into thin strips

3 bell peppers of any color, sliced into strips

1 onion (any color), sliced into strips

3 tablespoons (45 ml) extra-virgin olive oil

FAJITA SEASONING
¾ teaspoon salt

½ teaspoon chili powder

½ teaspoon onion powder

½ teaspoon garlic powder

½ teaspoon dried oregano

¼ teaspoon ground cumin

¼ teaspoon paprika

2 tablespoons (2 g) fresh cilantro or (8 g) parsley, chopped

1. Make the Steak & Vegetables: Move the oven rack to 5 to 6 inches (13 to 15 cm) from the broiler. Turn the broiler on high.

2. Spread the steak, bell peppers, and onion on a 12 x 17-inch (30 x 43 cm) baking sheet. Drizzle the oil over everything.

3. Make the Fajita Seasoning: In a small bowl, stir together the salt, chili powder, onion powder, garlic powder, oregano, cumin, and paprika. Sprinkle over everything on the baking sheet.

4. Use a spatula to move the steak, onions, and peppers around so that it's all coated with the Fajita Seasoning. Spread in an even layer.

5. Broil until the steak is done how you like it and the vegetables are tender, 7 to 8 minutes.

6. Remove from the oven and top with the fresh cilantro or parsley before serving.

TIP
- Enjoy as is or top with guacamole (pictured), salsa, or a squeeze of fresh lime juice.

balsamic basil chicken cauliflower rice bowls

Load up your dinner bowl with this mix of roasted veggies and balsamic chicken! This is the first sheet-pan recipe I ever posted on the blog, and it started my love affair with one-pan meals. It packs some big balsamic flavor that's not for the faint of heart.

PREP TIME 10 minutes
TOTAL TIME 30 minutes
MAKES 6 servings

1½ pounds (680 g) boneless, skinless chicken breasts, cut into 1-inch (2.5 cm) pieces

3 cups (213 g) broccoli florets, large florets halved

1 medium red onion, sliced into strips

2 cups (8 ounces, or 115 g) cauliflower rice

¼ cup (60 ml) plus 2 tablespoons (28 ml) balsamic vinegar, divided

3 tablespoons (45 ml) extra-virgin olive oil

1 tablespoon (10 g) minced garlic

Salt and black pepper to taste

2 tablespoons (5 g) chopped fresh basil

1. Preheat the oven to 425°F (220°C, or gas mark 7).

2. Spread the chicken in a single layer on one side of a 12 x 17-inch (30 x 43 cm) baking sheet. Add the broccoli florets beside your chicken. Spread the onion in a single layer beside the broccoli and add the cauliflower rice beside the onion. It's a lot, but it does all fit!

3. Drizzle ¼ cup (60 ml) of the vinegar and 3 tablespoons of oil over the chicken and broccoli. Top the chicken with the garlic.

4. Sprinkle salt and black pepper over everything on the baking sheet.

5. Bake for 15 minutes.

6. Remove from the oven and separate the chicken if it's sticking together. Drizzle the remaining 2 tablespoons (28 ml) vinegar over the chicken and top with the basil. Bake until the chicken is cooked through, completely opaque and juices run clear, about 5 additional minutes.

7. To serve, layer the cauliflower rice, red onion, broccoli, and chicken in bowls.

TIP

- Many people do not use olive oil when preparing this sheet pan meal to keep it extra light. You can omit if you prefer, but I'd recommend using parchment paper to help prevent sticking.

mediterranean fish dinner

For this recipe, I bake cod with classic Mediterranean ingredients like tomatoes, olives, and capers. Lemon brightens up this dish, and it's all a total feast for the eyes as well as the stomach!

PREP TIME 10 minutes
TOTAL TIME 30 minutes
MAKES 4 servings

2½ tablespoons (40 ml) extra-virgin olive oil

2 medium zucchini, halved and sliced into half-moons (about 4 cups, or 480 g)

4 cod fillets (6 ounces, or 170 g, each)

1 cup (180 g) grape tomatoes

¾ cup (75 g) pitted kalamata olives

2 tablespoons (18 g) capers

1 teaspoon minced garlic

1 teaspoon salt

½ teaspoon black pepper

1 lemon, thinly sliced

2 tablespoons (8 g) chopped fresh parsley

1. Preheat the oven to 425°F (220°C, or gas mark 7). Coat the bottom of a 9 x 13-inch (23 x 33 cm) baking dish with the oil.

2. Spread the zucchini across the bottom of the baking dish. Lay the cod on top so the fillets do not touch.

3. Place the tomatoes, olives, capers, and garlic on top of the zucchini in the spaces between the cod. Sprinkle the salt and black pepper over everything.

4. Place the lemon slices on top of the cod.

5. Bake until the fish is opaque and flakes easily with a fork and the zucchini is tender, 15 to 20 minutes. Garnish with the parsley before serving.

fajita chicken–stuffed bell peppers

Stuffed peppers are typically time-consuming and labor-intensive. I set out to make a version that is as fast as possible while still sticking with high-quality ingredients. To make that happen, I'm using a rotisserie chicken from the grocery store and a bag of steamed cauliflower rice from the freezer section. Since these two items are cooked before we stuff the peppers, everything else comes together quickly! It's a total weeknight dinner win.

PREP TIME 10 minutes

TOTAL TIME 30 minutes
+ rest time

MAKES 6 stuffed
bell peppers

6 bell peppers, any combination of colors

2½ cups (313 g) shredded cooked chicken

1 package (10 ounces, or 280 g) frozen cauliflower rice, steamed in the bag

1¼ cups (325 g) salsa

½ cup (90 g) chopped roasted red peppers

1½ teaspoons salt

1 teaspoon garlic powder

½ teaspoon chili powder

½ teaspoon black pepper

2 tablespoons (28 ml) extra-virgin olive oil

1. Preheat the oven to 450°F (230°C, or gas mark 8).

2. Cut the tops off the bell peppers and discard. Scoop out the seeds and ribs. Place the peppers upright in a baking dish that's just large enough to hold them.

3. In a large bowl, stir together the chicken, cauliflower rice, salsa, roasted red peppers, salt, garlic powder, chili powder, and black pepper.

4. Fill the peppers with the rice mixture. Drizzle the oil over the tops of your stuffed peppers.

5. Pour ½ cup (120 ml) water into the bottom of the baking dish. Bake for 10 minutes and then broil on high for 5 minutes more.

6. For more tender stuffed peppers, remove from the oven and cover with aluminum foil for 15 minutes before serving.

salisbury steaks with roasted sweet potatoes

This classic comfort food is now a one-pan meal complete with tender roasted sweet potatoes!

PREP TIME 15 minutes
TOTAL TIME 30 minutes
MAKES 4 servings

1½ tablespoons (25 ml) extra-virgin olive oil, divided

2 large sweet potatoes, diced into ½-inch (1 cm) cubes (about 4 cups, or 532 g)

1½ teaspoons salt, divided

1 pound (455 g) 93% lean ground beef

1 large egg

¼ cup (28 g) almond flour

¼ teaspoon, plus ⅛ teaspoon black pepper, divided

¼ teaspoon onion powder

¼ teaspoon garlic powder

1 medium white or yellow onion, thinly sliced

4 ounces (115 g) mushrooms, sliced

½ cup (120 ml) beef stock

2 teaspoons tomato paste

1 teaspoon minced garlic

1 teaspoon chopped fresh rosemary

1. Preheat the oven to 450°F (230°C, or gas mark 8).

2. Spread ½ tablespoon of the oil on half of a 12 x 17-inch (30 x 43 cm) sheet pan. Spread the sweet potatoes in a single layer on the side with the oil. Sprinkle with ¾ teaspoon of the salt. Drizzle the remaining 1 tablespoon (15 ml) oil on top of the potatoes.

3. In a large bowl, combine the ground beef, egg, almond flour, ½ teaspoon of the salt, ¼ teaspoon of the black pepper, onion powder, and garlic powder. Use your hands to mix together. Form four thin patties of the same size (about 4 x 4 inches [10 x 10 cm]) and place them on the ungreased half of the baking sheet. Add the onion around the patties. Add the mushrooms on top of the onion and patties.

4. In a small bowl, combine the stock, tomato paste, garlic, rosemary, the remaining ¼ teaspoon salt, and the remaining ⅛ teaspoon black pepper. Stir so that the tomato paste is thoroughly mixed in. Pour over the patties, onions, and mushrooms (not the potatoes).

5. Bake for 10 minutes and then broil on high until the beef is cooked through to a minimum internal temperature of 160°F (71°C) and the sweet potatoes are tender, 5 to 7 minutes.

halibut in tomato cream sauce

Layers of cauliflower rice, tomatoes, butternut squash, and halibut are topped with an easy tomato cream sauce for a dinner that looks as good as it tastes.

PREP TIME 10 minutes
TOTAL TIME 30 minutes
MAKES 4 servings

TOMATO CREAM SAUCE
1 can (28 ounces, or 785 g) crushed tomatoes

¾ cup (175 ml) canned unsweetened coconut milk, stirred

1½ teaspoons minced garlic

1 teaspoon salt

1 teaspoon dried oregano

1 teaspoon dried basil

½ teaspoon crushed red pepper flakes

½ teaspoon black pepper

HALIBUT & VEGGIES
2 packages (10 ounces, or 280 g, each) cauliflower rice, steamed

2 medium tomatoes, sliced ¼ inch (6 mm) thick

2 cups (280 g) diced butternut squash, 1-inch (2.5 cm) cubes (see Tip)

4 halibut fillets (6 ounces, or 170 g, each)

½ teaspoon salt

4 or 5 fresh basil leaves, chopped

1. Preheat the oven to 425°F (220°C, or gas mark 7).

2. Make the Tomato Cream Sauce: In a large bowl, combine the crushed tomatoes, coconut milk, garlic, salt, oregano, basil, red pepper flakes, and black pepper. Set aside.

3. Make the Halibut & Veggies: Spread the steamed cauliflower rice in the bottom of a 9 x 13-inch (23 x 33 cm) baking dish. Layer the tomatoes on top of the cauliflower and spread half of the Tomato Cream Sauce over the tomatoes. Layer the squash next and top with the halibut. Sprinkle the halibut with the salt and then spread the remaining sauce over everything.

4. Bake until the fish is opaque and flakes easily with a fork and the squash is tender, about 20 minutes. Garnish with the fresh basil before serving.

TIP
- Cut the butternut squash into cubes ¾ to 1 inch (2 to 2.5 cm) big. Some grocery stores carry pre-chopped squash in this very size. It's a huge time-saver!

baked chicken marsala

My sister has been asking me to create a chicken marsala recipe for years, so I can assure you there is no one more excited that I have turned it into a one-pan wonder than she is! While my version does not include any wine, I believe it does truly capture the flavor of a great chicken marsala. Plus, it cooks quickly, and you get asparagus too!

PREP TIME 5 minutes
TOTAL TIME 30 minutes
MAKES 4 servings

4 tablespoons 60 ml) extra-virgin olive oil, divided

1½ pounds (680 g) boneless, skinless chicken breasts, cut into 1-inch (2.5 cm) pieces

8 ounces (225 g) cremini or baby bella mushrooms, sliced

1 bunch asparagus, trimmed and cut into thirds

1 cup (235 ml) chicken stock

1½ tablespoons (25 ml) balsamic vinegar

1 tablespoon (10 g) minced garlic

½ teaspoon garlic powder

½ teaspoon onion powder

½ teaspoon black pepper

1½ teaspoons salt, divided

1 tablespoon (9 g) arrowroot flour

1 tablespoon (15 ml) cold water

1. Preheat the oven to 450°F (230°C, or gas mark 8).

2. Grease the bottom of a 9 x 13-inch (23 x 33 cm) baking dish with 1 tablespoon (15 ml) of the oil.

3. Place the chicken on one half of the baking dish. Top with the mushrooms. Add the asparagus to the remaining side of the dish. Pour the stock over everything.

4. Drizzle the remaining 3 tablespoons (45 ml) oil over all the ingredients. Add the vinegar, garlic, garlic powder, onion powder, black pepper, and 1 teaspoon of the salt to your mushrooms and chicken. Sprinkle the remaining ½ teaspoon salt over the asparagus.

5. Bake for 20 minutes. Remove from the oven. Remove the asparagus from the baking dish and set aside. Use a spatula to separate any chicken that's stuck together and spread it out in the baking dish. Return to the oven until the chicken is done, completely opaque and juices run clear, about 5 more minutes.

6. While the chicken is finishing in the oven, add the arrowroot flour and water to a small jar. Shake until well combined.

7. After baking, stir the slurry into the sauce. It will begin to thicken immediately. Then, stir the asparagus back in to coat in the sauce.

TIP
- I like to serve this dish over steamed cauliflower rice because then you can get more servings out of it!

harvest ranch chicken dinner

Ranch seasoning is so easy to make at home and packs so much flavor. In this recipe, we roast chicken, broccoli, carrots, and Brussels sprouts (lots of good veggies!) with this delectable seasoning. Everything gets coated, and the veggies come out perfectly tender with crispy edges. Just how I like them!

PREP TIME 10 minutes
TOTAL TIME 30 minutes
MAKES 4 to 6 servings

CHICKEN & VEGGIES

4 cups (284 g) broccoli florets

2 large carrots, peeled and cut into sticks (about 2 cups, or 244 g)

2 cups (176 g) Brussels sprouts, trimmed and halved

4 tablespoons (60 ml) extra-virgin olive oil, divided

1½ pounds (680 g) boneless, skinless chicken breasts, cut into 1-inch (2.5 cm) pieces

RANCH SEASONING

1 teaspoon dried dill

1 teaspoon dried parsley

1 teaspoon garlic powder

1 teaspoon salt

½ teaspoon onion powder

½ teaspoon black pepper

1. Make the Chicken & Veggies: Preheat the oven to 425°F (220°C, or gas mark 7). Line a 12 x 17-inch (30 x 43 cm) baking sheet with parchment paper.

2. Spread the broccoli, carrots, and Brussels sprouts in an even layer on the prepared baking sheet.

3. Drizzle 2 tablespoons (28 ml) of the oil over the veggies and bake for 5 minutes.

4. Meanwhile, make the Ranch Seasoning: In a small bowl, combine the dill, parsley, garlic powder, salt, onion powder, and black pepper.

5. Remove the pan from the oven and add the chicken. Drizzle the remaining 2 tablespoons (28 ml) oil over everything. Add all the Ranch Seasoning. Use a spatula to move the veggies and chicken around so that it's all well coated in oil and seasoning. Spread in a single layer.

6. Bake until the chicken is cooked through, completely opaque and juices run clear, and the vegetables are tender yet a little crispy, about 15 minutes.

TIP
- Feel free to swap out the chicken for boneless pork chops, cut into 1-inch (2.5 cm) pieces.

5

---

craveable skillet meals

It's hard to beat the easy cleanup and prep of
skillet meals. They're perfect for busy weeknights
because everything goes right in one pan—and
you can even serve dinner from it!

To accommodate all the ingredients in these recipes, I recommend using a nonstick skillet that's no smaller than 10 inches (25.5 cm) in diameter. One that's 11 or 12 inches (28 or 30 cm) will work best so that as much of your food as possible is touching the bottom of the pan. This allows for more even cooking.

Many of the recipes in this chapter feature chicken as the protein of choice because it's inexpensive, versatile, and generally enjoyed by the entire family (including children). You're welcome to swap pork for chicken, where noted, if that's your preference.

My favorite skillet-meal solution is always a great stir-fry. Protein and veggies in a delectable sauce . . . yes, please! Naturally, I have plenty of those for you in this chapter. But there's so much more you can make in a single skillet! How about a cauliflower rice bowl loaded with protein and veggies that tastes every bit as good as takeout? Or an incredible pad Thai made with butternut squash noodles? (Gasp! It's so good!) I bet you'll love salmon slathered in a maple glaze with the most tender sweet potatoes you've ever eaten. And let's not forget chicken stuffed with pizza ingredients and a poke bowl drizzled with spicy mayo. Honestly, I don't know how you're going to choose!

skillet chicken with summer vegetables

We always have way more squash and zucchini than I know what to do with by the end of summer. Our garden gives us an abundance, and it can get a bit out of hand! This skillet chicken is a delicious way to enjoy our favorite summer veggies. It's an easy dish made of fresh ingredients.

PREP TIME 10 minutes
TOTAL TIME 25 minutes
MAKES 2 to 4 servings

2 boneless, skinless chicken breasts (½ pound, or 225 g each)

2 teaspoons dried basil

1 teaspoon garlic powder, divided

1 teaspoon salt, divided

½ teaspoon onion powder

3 tablespoons (45 ml) extra-virgin olive oil or avocado oil, divided

2 yellow squash, halved and sliced into half-moons

2 medium zucchini, halved and sliced into half-moons

½ white or yellow onion, diced into ½-inch (1 cm) pieces

1 tablespoon (4 g) chopped fresh parsley

1. Slice the chicken horizontally to create four thin cutlets. Season all sides with the basil, ½ teaspoon of the garlic powder, ½ teaspoon of the salt, and onion powder.

2. Add 1 tablespoon (15 ml) of the oil to a skillet over medium-high heat. Place the cutlets in the hot pan. (You should hear a little sizzle.) Cook until browned, 3 to 4 minutes. Flip and brown the other side, another 3 to 4 minutes.

3. Carefully move the chicken to one side of the skillet and reduce the heat to medium. Add the remaining 2 tablespoons (28 ml) oil, squash, zucchini, and onion. Sprinkle with the remaining ½ teaspoon salt and remaining ½ teaspoon garlic powder. Cover and simmer, stirring the veggies occasionally, until the vegetables are tender and the chicken is cooked through to a minimum internal temperature of 165°F (74°C), 5 to 7 minutes. (If using pork cutlets, cook to a minimum internal temperature of 145°F [63°C].)

4. Garnish with the parsley before serving. Taste and add salt, if desired.

TIP
- Swap out the chicken for thin-sliced pork cutlets, if you like.

fiesta pineapple chicken

This easy stir-fry of chicken, pineapple, and vegetables is the perfect combination of sweet and savory. It's also so pretty, if I do say so myself!

PREP TIME 10 minutes
TOTAL TIME 25 minutes
MAKES 4 servings

2 tablespoons (28 ml) extra-virgin olive oil or avocado oil

1 pound (455 g) boneless, skinless chicken breasts, cut into 1-inch (2.5 cm) pieces

1 red bell pepper, cut into 1-inch (2.5 cm) pieces

½ white or yellow onion, cut into 1-inch (2.5 cm) pieces

12 ounces (340 g) green beans, trimmed and halved

¾ teaspoon salt

½ teaspoon black pepper

½ teaspoon ground ginger

1 can (14 ounces, or 390 g) pineapple chunks, drained, or 1½ cups (250 g) fresh

½ cup (120 ml) chicken stock

¼ cup (60 ml) coconut aminos

1½ teaspoons minced garlic

¼ teaspoon crushed red pepper flakes

1 tablespoon (9 g) arrowroot flour

1 tablespoon (15 ml) cold water

1. Add the oil to the skillet over medium-high heat. Once hot, add the chicken. Sauté, flipping occasionally to brown all sides of the chicken, about 3 to 5 minutes, using a spatula to separate the pieces when they get stuck together. Remove the chicken from the skillet and set aside.

2. Add the bell pepper, onion, and green beans to the skillet. Sauté, stirring occasionally, until the onion is tender and the bell pepper and green beans have some browning, about 5 minutes.

3. Add the chicken back to your skillet along with the salt, black pepper, and ginger. Stir in the pineapple chunks.

4. Stir in the stock, coconut aminos, garlic, and red pepper flakes. Simmer for 2 to 3 minutes until the chicken is cooked through, completely opaque and juices run clear, and everything is warmed through.

5. Turn off the stove. To thicken the sauce, combine the arrowroot flour and water in a small jar. Shake vigorously and pour the slurry into the skillet and stir. The sauce will begin to thicken immediately.

6. Taste and add more salt and black pepper, if desired.

20-minute skillet sausage & zucchini

Throw together this quick skillet dinner when you need a healthy and satisfying meal in a hurry! You'll love this perfectly seasoned mix of sausage, zucchini, peppers, and onions.

PREP TIME 10 minutes
TOTAL TIME 20 minutes
MAKES 4 servings

2½ tablespoons (40 ml) extra-virgin olive oil or avocado oil, divided

4 fully cooked sausages, sliced into circles ¼ inch (6 mm) thick

2 medium zucchini, diced into 1-inch (2 cm) pieces

1 white or yellow onion, diced into 1-inch (2 cm) pieces

1 bell pepper, any color, diced into 1-inch (2 cm) pieces

½ teaspoon salt

½ teaspoon dried oregano

½ teaspoon dried basil

¼ teaspoon garlic powder

¼ teaspoon onion powder

¼ teaspoon black pepper

1 teaspoon minced garlic

Fresh chopped basil, for garnish (optional)

1. Add 1 tablespoon (15 ml) of the oil to a skillet over medium-high heat. Once hot, add the sliced sausage. Sautè, flipping the sausage frequently, until the sausage has some browning, 2 to 3 minutes. Remove from the pan and set aside.

2. Reduce the heat to medium. Add the remaining 1½ tablespoons (25 ml) of oil to the skillet with the zucchini, onion, and bell pepper. Sprinkle with the salt, oregano, basil, garlic powder, onion powder, and black pepper. Stir. Sautè until the onion is translucent and the peppers and zucchini are close to tender, about 5 minutes.

3. Return the sausage to the skillet along with the minced garlic. Stir. Cover so everything heats through for 1 to 2 minutes. Taste and add more salt, if desired. Garnish with chopped fresh basil, if desired.

ghee chicken with sweet sautéed carrots

How about a simple and easy-to-throw-together dinner? First, we'll sauté our chicken thighs in ghee until they're deliciously browned. Add in some tender, honeyed carrots, and you're all done. The nuttiness of the ghee beautifully complements the sweetness of the carrots for a delicious meal!

PREP TIME 5 minutes
TOTAL TIME 20 minutes
MAKES 4 servings

1½ **pounds (680 g) boneless, skinless chicken thighs**

½ **teaspoon salt**

½ **teaspoon garlic powder**

3 **tablespoons (42 g) ghee, divided**

1 **pound (455 g) carrots, peeled and sliced ¼ inch (6 mm) thick**

1 **tablespoon (20 g) raw honey**

1. Pat the chicken thighs dry. Rub the salt and garlic powder into the top of the chicken.

2. Place 1 tablespoon (14 g) of the ghee in a skillet over medium-high heat. Once hot, add the chicken, seasoned-side down. (You should hear a sizzle.) Flip once you see a beautiful brown on the side of the chicken in the pan, 3 to 4 minutes. Brown the other side, about another 3 minutes. The chicken will not be completely cooked through at this point.

3. Reduce the heat to medium. Use a spatula to move the chicken to one side of the pan. Add the carrots, 3 tablespoons (45 ml) water, honey, and remaining 2 tablespoons (28 g) ghee. Cover and simmer until the carrots are tender and the chicken is cooked through to a minimum internal temperature of 165°F (74°C), 5 to 7 minutes. Taste and add more salt, if desired.

TIP
- Feel free to swap out the chicken thighs for chicken breasts. Breasts generally require less overall cooking time, depending on the thickness.

paleo tuna poke

This is likely my husband's favorite recipe. It is super simple to throw together and so ridiculously flavorful! The only cooking this dish requires is in preparing the cauliflower rice. Here, I'm showing you how to steam it in a skillet, but you are welcome to buy the cauliflower rice that steams in a bag and use that to further simplify things. This recipe is made to feed one person (it's a generous serving), so double it or triple it depending on how many you are serving.

PREP TIME 15 minutes
TOTAL TIME 20 minutes
MAKES 1 serving

CAULIFLOWER RICE
2 cups (8 ounces, or 225 g) cauliflower rice

1 tablespoon (15 ml) extra-virgin olive oil

Salt and black pepper, to taste

SPICY MAYO
2 tablespoons (28 g) mayo

1 teaspoon sriracha or hot sauce

TUNA & VEGGIES & SESAME-SOY SAUCE
3 ounces (85 g) sushi-grade tuna, cut into ½-inch (1 cm) cubes

½ cup (70 g) diced cucumber, ½-inch (1 cm) cubes

¼ cup (35 g) shredded purple cabbage

¼ cup (28 g) grated carrot

¼ cup (21 g) microgreens

3 tablespoons (45 ml) coconut aminos

1½ teaspoons extra-virgin olive oil

1 teaspoon rice vinegar

½ avocado, sliced
Sesame seeds, for garnish

1. Make the Cauliflower Rice: Add the cauliflower to a skillet over medium heat with the oil. Cover with a lid so the cauliflower steams until tender, 4 to 5 minutes. (If you're doubling or tripling this recipe, your cauliflower will take a few more minutes to cook.) Add salt and black pepper, to taste.

2. Meanwhile, prepare the Spicy Mayo: In a small bowl, stir together the mayo and sriracha or hot sauce.

3. Make the Tuna & Veggies & Sesame-Soy Sauce: In a medium bowl, gently toss together the tuna, cucumber, cabbage, carrots, and microgreens. Drizzle the coconut aminos, oil, and vinegar over the top. Stir so everything is coated.

4. To serve, layer the cauliflower rice in the bottom of a bowl. Top with your tuna and veggie mixture. Add your Spicy Mayo and sliced avocado on top. Now, garnish with sesame seeds.

chicken squash skillet

Fresh zucchini and butternut squash make this skillet meal a celebration of fall veggies. Swap out the chicken for pork tenderloin, if you like, and serve it all over cauliflower rice to take full advantage of the sauce.

PREP TIME 10 minutes
TOTAL TIME 25 minutes
MAKES 4 servings

1½ tablespoons (25 ml) extra-virgin olive oil or avocado oil

1 yellow or orange bell pepper, cut into strips

½ white or yellow onion, cut into strips

1 teaspoon minced garlic

1 pound (455 g) boneless, skinless chicken breasts, cut into thin pieces

2 medium zucchini, halved and sliced into half-moons (about 3 cups, or 360 g)

2 cups (280 g) diced butternut squash, 1-inch (2.5 cm) cubes (see Tip)

¾ cup (175 ml) chicken stock

¼ cup (60 ml) coconut aminos

1 tablespoon (15 ml) rice vinegar

¾ teaspoon salt

½ teaspoon black pepper

¼ teaspoon ground ginger

¼ teaspoon crushed red pepper flakes

1. Add the oil to a large skillet over medium-high heat. Once hot, add the bell pepper and onion. Sauté until the pepper has a bit of browning and the onion is tender, 3 to 4 minutes. Add the garlic and sauté for another minute so the garlic is golden in color. Remove from the pan and set aside.

2. Add the chicken to the skillet. (If needed, drizzle in another tablespoon [15 ml] oil.) Sauté, stirring frequently, until the chicken is nicely browned, about 3 minutes. It doesn't need to be fully cooked through at this point; we're just adding a bit of color to our chicken.

3. Add the zucchini, butternut squash, stock, coconut aminos, vinegar, salt, black pepper, ginger, red pepper flakes, and the cooked bell pepper and onion to the skillet. Stir. Reduce the heat to medium, cover, and simmer until the zucchini and squash are tender and the chicken is cooked through, completely opaque and juices run clear, 5 to 10 minutes. Taste and add more salt and black pepper, if desired.

TIP
• While I always slice up my own zucchini and yellow squash, I'm a big fan of purchasing the cubed butternut squash from the grocery store. It saves some trouble and time. Plus, butternut squash can be fairly large, and I rarely want to use an entire squash of that size. Whether to chop or not is totally your call!

stuffed pizza chicken with veggies

Stuff your chicken breasts with a mix of mushrooms, bell pepper, and diced pepperoni to emulate a supreme pizza. It looks impressive, especially when paired with sautéed green beans!

PREP TIME 10 minutes
TOTAL TIME 30 minutes
MAKES 4 servings

CHICKEN
4 boneless, skinless chicken breasts (½ pound, or 225 g, each)

2 tablespoons (28 ml) extra-virgin olive oil or avocado oil, plus more for drizzling

1½ tablespoons (9 g) Italian seasoning

¾ teaspoon salt

PIZZA FILLING
1 tablespoon (15 ml) extra-virgin olive oil or avocado oil

½ cup (35 g) chopped fresh mushrooms

½ cup (75 g) diced bell pepper of any color, ½-inch (1 cm) pieces

30 pieces pepperoni (about 2 ounces, or 55 g), diced

GREEN BEANS
2 tablespoons (28 ml) extra-virgin olive oil or avocado oil

12 ounces (340 g) green beans, trimmed

¼ teaspoon salt

1. Make the Chicken: Slice each chicken breast on the side, about halfway through, to create a pocket for the stuffing. Drizzle a little oil all over the chicken breasts and sprinkle with the Italian seasoning and salt.

2. Make the Pizza Filling: Add the oil to a large skillet over medium-high heat. Once hot, add the mushrooms and bell pepper. Sauté, stirring occasionally, until the peppers soften and have some browning, 3 to 5 minutes.

3. Transfer the mushrooms and bell peppers to a small bowl and stir in the pepperoni. Set aside.

4. Add 2 tablespoons (28 ml) oil to the skillet and return to medium-high heat. Carefully stuff the filling inside the chicken pockets. Place in the skillet, top-side down. Let the chicken cook undisturbed until golden brown, 2 to 3 minutes. Flip and cook until the other side is browned, another 2 to 3 minutes. The chicken will not be cooked through at this point. Remove the chicken from the skillet and set aside.

5. Make the Green Beans: Add the oil to your skillet along with the green beans. Reduce the heat to medium. Cook, stirring occasionally, until they start to soften and you see some browning, 5 to 7 minutes. Sprinkle with the salt.

6. Use a spatula or tongs to gently move the green beans to one side of the skillet. Add the chicken back to the skillet beside the green beans. Cover and cook for 5 to 10 minutes, or until the chicken is cooked through.

7. Check to make sure the chicken is cooked through to a minimum internal temperature of 165°F (74°C). Taste and add more salt or black pepper, if desired.

orange-balsamic chicken with broccoli

Orange and balsamic are a fun and surprising flavor combination that I can't get enough of. It all started with a recipe I made a few years ago for orange-balsamic chicken wings, and my immensely popular orange-balsamic meatballs came next. Now, I'm letting that duo shine in this quick chicken and broccoli stir-fry. If you prefer pork tenderloin or boneless pork chops, they'd make a fine substitute for the chicken.

PREP TIME 10 minutes
TOTAL TIME 20 minutes
MAKES 2 servings

2 tablespoons (28 ml)
extra-virgin olive oil
or avocado oil

1½ pounds (680 g) boneless,
skinless chicken breasts, cut
into 1-inch (2.5 cm) pieces

Zest from 1 orange

½ cup (120 ml)
fresh orange juice

2 tablespoons (28 ml)
pure maple syrup

2 tablespoons (28 ml)
balsamic vinegar

1 teaspoon tomato paste

1 teaspoon salt

½ teaspoon ground ginger

½ teaspoon garlic powder

½ teaspoon black pepper

12 ounces (340 g)
broccoli florets

1. Add the oil to a skillet over medium-high heat. Once hot, add the chicken. Sauté, stirring frequently, until the chicken is nicely browned and cooked through, completely opaque and juices run clear, 3 to 5 minutes. It cooks quickly because it's been cut into small pieces.

2. Add the zest, orange juice, maple syrup, vinegar, tomato paste, salt, ginger, garlic powder, and black pepper to the skillet. Stir to combine. Now, add the broccoli. Cover and let your broccoli steam until it's how you like it, usually 2 to 3 minutes to keep it bright with a little crispiness.

3. Once done simmering, turn off the heat and uncover. Let sit for 2 minutes to cook off a bit of the sauce. Taste and add more salt and black pepper, if desired.

garlic-lemon halibut with sautéed asparagus

Halibut has a mild flavor that pleases pretty much everybody. (Even those who protest that they don't really enjoy seafood.) My favorite way to dress it up is with a lovely sauce of ghee, lemon juice, garlic, and thyme. It's just perfect with asparagus!

PREP TIME 5 minutes
TOTAL TIME 10 minutes
MAKES 4 servings

HALIBUT & ASPARAGUS
**4 halibut fillets
(6 ounces, or 170 g, each)**

Salt and black pepper

**2 tablespoons (28 ml)
extra-virgin olive oil**

1 bunch asparagus, trimmed

GARLIC-LEMON SAUCE
¼ cup (56 g) ghee, melted

**2 tablespoons (28 ml)
 fresh lemon juice**

**1 tablespoon (2 g)
chopped fresh thyme**

1 teaspoon minced garlic

1. Make the Halibut & Asparagus: Generously sprinkle the top and bottom of the halibut with salt and black pepper.

2. Add the oil to a large skillet over medium-high heat. Once hot, carefully add each fillet with the presentation-side down. Place the asparagus beside the fish and sprinkle with salt. We want a beautiful golden color on the side of the halibut that's touching the bottom of the pan, so don't flip it until you've achieved that color, 4 to 5 minutes.

3. Meanwhile, make the Garlic-Lemon Sauce: Stir together the ghee, lemon juice, thyme, and garlic in a small bowl.

4. Carefully flip your halibut and use your spatula or tongs to move the asparagus around so all the stalks get a turn at the bottom of the pan.

5. Reduce the heat to medium-low or low. Pour your ghee mixture over the halibut and asparagus. Cover and let the halibut cook through until it is opaque and flakes easily with a fork, 3 to 4 minutes.

6. To serve, divide the asparagus among plates and top with the halibut. Drizzle a bit of the sauce from the pan over the fish.

spanish chicken

My obsession with ghee is real and has been going for 5+ years! It is my go-to cooking fat for chicken because it adds a hint of sweetness and helps everything brown beautifully. It's the ghee, along with the bold flavors in the dry rub, that make this chicken extra delicious.

PREP TIME 10 minutes
TOTAL TIME 25 minutes
MAKES 2 to 4 servings

DRY RUB

1 teaspoon paprika

¾ teaspoon salt

½ teaspoon garlic powder

½ teaspoon onion powder

½ teaspoon ground cumin

½ teaspoon chili powder

CHICKEN & VEGGIES

2 boneless, skinless chicken breasts (½ pound, or 225 g, each)

2½ tablespoons (35 g) ghee, divided

8 ounces (225 g) green beans, trimmed

Handful of cherry tomatoes

½ teaspoon salt

1. Make the Dry Rub: Combine the paprika, salt, garlic powder, onion powder, cumin, and chili powder in a small bowl.

2. Make the Chicken & Veggies: Slice the chicken horizontally to create four thin cutlets. Press the Dry Rub into the top of the cutlets.

3. Add 1½ tablespoons (21 g) of the ghee to a skillet over medium-high heat. Once hot, add the chicken, seasoned-side down. (You should hear a little sizzle.) Cook until browned, 3 to 4 minutes. Flip and brown the other side, another 3 to 4 minutes. Your seasoned side will have significantly more browning thanks to that incredible dry rub.

4. Carefully move the chicken to one side of the skillet and reduce the heat to medium. Add the remaining 1 tablespoon (14 g) ghee, green beans, and tomatoes to the other side of the skillet. Add the salt to the veggies. Cover and simmer until the chicken is cooked through, completely opaque and juices run clear, and the green beans are tender with some crunch, 5 to 10 minutes.

skillet chicken & brussels sprouts

Whip up this simple stir-fry of chicken and Brussels sprouts any night of the week in only 25 minutes! It sautés in an easy sauce of coconut aminos, rice vinegar, garlic, and crushed red pepper flakes to infuse every bite with big flavor. Feel free to swap the chicken with pork tenderloin.

PREP TIME 10 minutes
TOTAL TIME 25 minutes
MAKES 2 to 4 servings

1½ tablespoons (25 ml) extra-virgin olive oil or avocado oil

1½ pounds (680 g) boneless, skinless chicken breasts, cut into 1-inch (2.5 cm) pieces

1 pound (455 g) Brussels sprouts, trimmed and halved

Salt and black pepper

½ cup (120 ml) coconut aminos

1 tablespoon (15 ml) rice vinegar or apple cider vinegar

1 tablespoon (10 g) minced garlic

¼ to ½ teaspoon crushed red pepper flakes

1. Add the oil to a large skillet over medium-high heat. Once hot, add the chicken and Brussels sprouts. Sprinkle with salt and black pepper. Sauté for 3 to 4 minutes, stirring occasionally. The chicken should be close to done with some color, and the Brussels sprouts will have a bit of brown. Use a spatula to gently separate the chicken that gets stuck together.

2. Stir in the coconut aminos, vinegar, garlic, and red pepper flakes. Reduce the heat to medium and cover. Simmer until the Brussels sprouts are softened and the chicken is cooked all the way through, completely opaque and juices run clear, 5 to 6 minutes.

3. Turn off the heat and uncover. Let sit for 2 minutes to cook off a bit of the sauce. Taste and add extra salt or black pepper, if desired.

TIP
- This is a delicious meal on its own, but if you'd like to make it even heartier, simply serve it over steamed cauliflower rice or roasted veggies and potatoes.

crispy chicken thighs with greens

Get your greens in this simple dish of lightly spiced chicken thighs and garlicky spinach. You can swap out the spinach for any other fast-cooking green veggie and make this seem like a new dish every time you make it!

PREP TIME 5 minutes
TOTAL TIME 20 minutes
MAKES 4 servings

CHICKEN THIGHS
½ teaspoon salt

½ teaspoon chili powder

½ teaspoon garlic powder

½ teaspoon black pepper

¼ teaspoon curry powder

¼ teaspoon paprika

1½ pounds (680 g) boneless, skinless chicken thighs

1½ tablespoons (21 g) ghee (see Tip)

SPINACH
½ to 1½ teaspoons extra-virgin olive oil

15 ounces (425 g) fresh baby spinach (see Tip)

1½ teaspoons minced garlic

½ teaspoon salt

1. Make the Chicken Thighs: In a small bowl, stir together the salt, chili powder, garlic powder, black pepper, curry powder, and paprika.

2. Pat the chicken thighs dry. Rub the spice mixture into the top of the chicken.

3. Place the ghee in a skillet over medium-high heat. Once hot, add the chicken, seasoned-side down. (You should hear a sizzle.) Flip once you see a beautiful brown on the side of the chicken in the pan, 5 minutes. Brown the other side, another 6 to 7 minutes. Remove the chicken from the pan and set aside.

4. Make the Spinach: Reduce the heat to medium. Assess how much fat remains in the skillet. You may find that you don't need to add any oil, or you may only need a little. Add the oil (if needed), spinach, garlic, and salt. Stir until all the spinach fits. Place the chicken thighs on top of the spinach. Cover and simmer until the chicken is cooked through to a minimum internal temperature of 165°F (74°C) and the spinach is wilted, 2 to 4 minutes.

TIP
- Use another cooking fat in place of ghee if you like. I personally really enjoy the rich flavor of ghee for sautéing chicken.

- Interested in using something other than spinach? Mustard greens cook quickly, so they're a great swap; tear or chop the greens into large pieces before sautéing. If you'd like to use kale, remove the thickest part of the stems first and then give the leaves a rough chop; cook kale for 6 to 8 minutes. Broccoli cooks fast, too; just move those thighs to the side of your skillet, add the broccoli, and cover and cook until it's how you like it!

alfredo chicken & zoodles

A creamy yet dairy-free alfredo sauce makes this dish really shine. The nutritional yeast gives it that cheesy flavor, while the cashews make it silky and lush. With chicken, asparagus, and zoodles, this is one comfort food that's actually light!

PREP TIME 15 minutes
+ cashew soak time
TOTAL TIME 30 minutes
MAKES 4 servings

ALFREDO SAUCE
1 cup (140 g) raw cashews (see Tip)

1½ tablespoons (25 ml) extra-virgin olive oil

½ white onion, diced into ½-inch (1 cm) pieces

1 tablespoon (10 g) minced garlic

1½ tablespoons (25 ml) fresh lemon juice

1 tablespoon (4 g) nutritional yeast

1 teaspoon salt

½ teaspoon black pepper

CHICKEN & ASPARAGUS
2 tablespoons (28 ml) extra-virgin olive oil or avocado oil

1 pound (455 g) boneless, skinless chicken breasts, cut into 1-inch (2.5 cm) pieces

½ bunch asparagus, trimmed and cut into thirds

½ teaspoon salt

ZOODLES
4 medium zucchini, or 20 ounces (560 g) store-bought zoodles

1. Make the Alfredo Sauce: Soak the cashews in water to cover for at least 1 hour. Drain the water when you're ready to cook.

2. Add the oil to a skillet over medium-high heat. Once hot, add the onion. Sauté until tender, 3 to 4 minutes. Add the garlic and sauté until golden, another minute.

3. Transfer the mixture to a high-powered blender or food processor, along with the soaked cashews, ¾ cup (175 ml) water, the lemon juice, nutritional yeast, salt, and black pepper. Blend until smooth. Taste and add more salt or black pepper, if desired.

4. Make the Chicken & Asparagus: Add the oil to the skillet over medium-high heat. Sauté the chicken to brown all sides, about 3 minutes, using a spatula to separate the pieces when they get stuck together. Add the asparagus and sauté until the asparagus is crisp tender and the chicken is cooked through, about 3 minutes. Add the salt to the chicken and asparagus.

5. Meanwhile, prepare your Zoodles: Make zucchini noodles from the zucchini using a spiralizer according to the manufacturer's directions.

6. Reduce the heat to medium-low. Pour your Alfredo Sauce into the skillet. Use tongs to stir in the zoodles, cover, and simmer until the zoodles are how you like them. This can take as little as 2 minutes, if you're using the thin store-bought zoodles, or as long as 5 minutes, if you make your own thick zoodles (my preference).

TIP
- To soften cashews quickly, add the cashews to a bowl, add water to cover, and microwave for about 1 minute.

lemon shrimp stir-fry

Dinner in 20 minutes? This is the stir-fry for you! Shrimp, bell pepper, broccoli, and snow peas simmer in a flavorful lemon sauce. It's so delicious and easy!

PREP TIME 10 minutes
TOTAL TIME 20 minutes
MAKES 4 servings

LEMON SAUCE
⅔ cup (160 ml) vegetable stock

¼ cup (60 ml) fresh lemon juice

1½ teaspoons minced garlic

1½ teaspoons chopped fresh rosemary

1 teaspoon coconut aminos

¼ teaspoon rice vinegar

¼ teaspoon crushed red pepper flakes

¼ teaspoon salt

¼ teaspoon black pepper

SHRIMP STIR-FRY
1 pound (455 g) peeled and deveined shrimp (16 to 20 count)

Salt and black pepper

2 tablespoons (28 ml) extra-virgin olive oil

1 red bell pepper, sliced into strips

1 yellow or orange bell pepper, sliced into strips

12 ounces (340 g) broccoli florets

8 ounces (225 g) snow peas or fresh green beans (see Tip)

Lemon zest, for garnish (optional)

Fresh chopped parsley, for garnish (optional)

1. Make the Lemon Sauce: Whisk together the stock, lemon juice, garlic, rosemary, coconut aminos, vinegar, red pepper flakes, salt, and black pepper in a small bowl. Set aside.

2. Make the Shrimp Stir-Fry: Sprinkle the shrimp with salt and black pepper.

3. Add the oil to a large skillet over medium-high heat. When hot, add the bell peppers and broccoli. Sauté, stirring frequently, until the peppers have started to soften and you're getting some browning, 4 to 5 minutes.

4. Pour the Lemon Sauce into the skillet and add the shrimp. Carefully stir so everything is well combined. Place the snow peas on top. (Do not stir or the peas will turn to mush.) Cover and simmer until the shrimp is curled and no longer pink, 2 to 3 minutes.

5. Garnish with lemon zest and parsley before serving, if desired.

TIP
- If using green beans instead of snow peas, add them to the skillet with the bell peppers and broccoli. They'll take longer to cook than the snow peas, which are very thin and require minimal cooking time.

beef & broccoli

This beef and broccoli is faster than takeout and so much healthier too! This dish is packed with tender strips of sirloin in an easy marinade and crunchy broccoli florets. The marinade works its magic in as little as 15 minutes, but you can get the meat going in the morning, if you prefer, and then you'll be ready to cook at dinnertime. The whole family will adore this one! It's hearty enough as is, but enjoy it over steamed cauliflower rice for an even more satisfying meal.

PREP TIME 10 minutes
+ marinating time
TOTAL TIME 20 minutes
MAKES 4 servings

MARINADE & BEEF
⅓ cup (80 ml) coconut aminos

1 teaspoon minced garlic

1 teaspoon ground ginger

½ teaspoon salt

½ teaspoon black pepper

½ teaspoon garlic powder

½ teaspoon onion powder

1 pound (455 g) sirloin or flank steak, cut into thin strips

2 tablespoons (28 ml) extra-virgin olive oil

BROCCOLI
1 pound (455 g) broccoli florets

Salt and black pepper

1 scallion, sliced, for garnish (optional)

1½ teaspoons sesame seeds, for garnish (optional)

Coconut aminos, for drizzling (optional)

1. Make the Marinade & Beef: In a resealable plastic bag or bowl, combine the coconut aminos, garlic, ginger, salt, black pepper, garlic powder, and onion powder. Add the steak, seal the bag, and toss to coat. Refrigerate for a minimum of 15 minutes and up to 12 hours before cooking.

2. Add the oil to a skillet over medium-high heat. Once hot, add the steak in a single layer. (Reserve any marinade that hasn't been absorbed.) Sauté the steak so that all the sides get a bit of crispy browning, about 5 minutes. The beef doesn't need to be completely cooked through before moving to the next step.

3. Make the Broccoli: Reduce the heat to medium. Add the broccoli, any leftover marinade, ½ cup (120 ml) water, salt, and black pepper. Stir. Cover and let the broccoli steam until it's how you like it, usually 2 to 3 minutes to keep it bright with a little crispiness.

4. Taste and add extra salt or black pepper, if necessary. Top with scallion, sesame seeds, and/or an extra drizzle of coconut aminos before serving, if desired.

honey chicken & green beans

I could lick this honey sauce right out of the bowl, but instead, I decided to slather it over breaded chunks of chicken and sautéed green beans. You'll want to use a large skillet so you have enough space to accommodate both the chicken and the green beans.

PREP TIME 15 minutes
TOTAL TIME 30 minutes
MAKES 4 servings

CHICKEN
¾ cup (84 g) finely ground almond flour

¾ teaspoon salt

½ teaspoon garlic powder

¼ teaspoon chili powder

¼ teaspoon dried parsley

¼ teaspoon dried basil

1 large egg

1 pound (455 g) boneless, skinless chicken breasts, cut into chunks (smaller than nuggets)

2 to 3 tablespoons (28 to 45 ml) olive oil or avocado oil

HONEY SAUCE
½ cup (170 g) raw honey

1½ cups (355 ml) coconut aminos

GREEN BEANS
2 tablespoons (28 ml) extra-virgin olive oil or avocado oil

12 ounces (340 g) green beans, trimmed

1 teaspoon minced garlic

¼ teaspoon salt

1. Make the Chicken: Add the almond flour, salt, garlic powder, chili powder, parsley, and basil to a shallow dish. Stir to combine.

2. Whisk the egg in a small bowl.

3. Dredge each chicken piece in the egg mixture and let the excess drip off. Then, dredge each in the breading mixture.

4. Heat 2 tablespoons (28 ml) of the oil in a skillet over medium-high heat. The oil should cover the bottom of the skillet, so add another tablespoon (15 ml), if needed.

5. Once hot, add the chicken and fry on each side until golden brown and cooked through, completely opaque and juices run clear, about 5 minutes. Remove from the pan to a paper towel–lined plate. Drain the oil and wipe the inside of the skillet clean.

6. Meanwhile, make your Honey Sauce: Combine the honey and coconut aminos in a small bowl and set aside.

7. Make the Green Beans: Add the oil to your skillet and return to medium-high heat. When hot, add the green beans. Cook, stirring occasionally, until they're soft and you start to see that browning we want, 5 to 7 minutes. Stir in the garlic and salt and sauté for another minute.

8. Return the chicken to the pan. Pour the sauce over your chicken and green beans. Stir everything together so that the sauce is coating every delicious bite. Reduce the heat to medium-low, cover, and let it all simmer to warm through, 1 to 2 minutes.

TIP
- To bread your chicken, lay the chicken on top of the breading ingredients. Use fingers your to cover the top with breading and press it into the chicken. Breading will stick to the bottom while you do this.

maple salmon with sweet potatoes

You will not believe what the maple syrup does to the salmon and sweet potatoes in this impressive meal. I swear these are the sweetest, most tender potatoes I've ever had. I can't wait for you to try this showstopper of a dish!

PREP TIME 10 minutes
TOTAL TIME 30 minutes
MAKES 4 servings

SWEET POTATOES
2 tablespoons (28 g) coconut oil

2 medium sweet potatoes, diced into ¼-inch (6 mm) cubes

½ teaspoon ground cinnamon

⅛ teaspoon salt, plus more to taste

SALMON
4 wild-caught salmon fillets (6 ounces, or 170 g, each)

Black pepper, to taste

1 tablespoon (14 g) ghee

MAPLE SAUCE
¼ cup (60 ml) pure maple syrup

3 tablespoons (45 ml) coconut aminos

2 teaspoons ghee, melted

1 teaspoon minced garlic

1. Make the Sweet Potatoes: Add the oil to a skillet over medium-high heat. Once hot, add the sweet potatoes, cinnamon, and ⅛ teaspoon of salt. Stir frequently as you sauté for 4 to 5 minutes. Then, cover and cook until softened, another 4 to 5 minutes.

2. Meanwhile, make the Salmon: Pat the salmon dry. (This will help the skin crisp up as it cooks and will reduce the likelihood of it sticking to the pan.) Sprinkle with salt and black pepper.

3. Use a spatula to carefully move the sweet potatoes to one side of the skillet. Add the ghee to the empty side. Place the salmon in the ghee, skin-side up. Cook until golden brown on the side pressed into the pan, about 4 minutes.

4. While the salmon is cooking, make the Maple Sauce: Stir together the maple syrup, coconut aminos, melted ghee, and garlic in a small bowl.

5. Gently flip the salmon. Pour your Maple Sauce over everything. Cook until the fish is firm to the touch, opaque, and flakes easily with a fork, about 3 minutes.

salsa chicken & mexican cauliflower rice

Lighten up your dinner with this sautéed chicken topped with homemade pico de gallo. Serve it on a bed of Mexican cauliflower rice, and your family will thank you!

PREP TIME 10 minutes
TOTAL TIME 30 minutes
MAKES 2 to 4 servings

CHICKEN
2 boneless, skinless chicken breasts (½ pound, or 225 g, each)

1 teaspoon dried oregano

½ teaspoon salt

½ teaspoon onion powder

½ teaspoon garlic powder

2 tablespoons (28 ml) extra-virgin olive oil

PICO DE GALLO
1 medium tomato, diced into ½-inch (1 cm) or smaller pieces

½ large onion, diced into ½-inch (1 cm) or smaller pieces

¼ to ½ small jalapeño, seeded and diced (optional)

Handful of cilantro, chopped

Lime juice, to taste

Salt, to taste

MEXICAN CAULIFLOWER RICE
¼ cup (38 g) diced red bell pepper, ½-inch (1 cm) dice

¼ cup (38 g) diced green bell pepper, ½-inch (1 cm) dice

¼ white or yellow onion, diced into ½-inch (1 cm) pieces

1 teaspoon minced garlic

3 cups (12 ounces, or 340 g) fresh or frozen cauliflower rice

2 teaspoons fresh lime juice

½ teaspoon salt

¼ teaspoon chili powder

1. Make the Chicken: Slice the chicken horizontally to create four thin cutlets. Mix the oregano, salt, onion powder, and garlic powder in a small bowl and press the mixture into the top of the chicken.

2. Add the oil to a skillet over medium-high heat. Place the chicken, seasoned-side down, in the hot pan. (You should hear a sizzle!) Cook until browned, 3 to 4 minutes. Flip and brown the other side, another 3 minutes. Remove the chicken from the pan and set aside. The chicken does not need to be completely cooked through.

3. Meanwhile, assemble the Pico de Gallo: In a bowl, stir together the tomato, onion, jalapeño (if using), and cilantro. Add the lime juice and salt a little at a time until you get it how you like it. Set aside.

4. Make the Mexican Cauliflower Rice: To the skillet, add the bell peppers, onion, and garlic and return to medium-high heat. Scrape up the browned chicken bits remaining in the pan. You should have enough fat left in the pan to sauté with, but if you need more, add an extra tablespoon (15 ml) oil. Sauté until the peppers and onion start to get tender, 2 to 3 minutes.

5. Stir in the cauliflower rice. Add the lime juice, salt, chili powder, and 3 tablespoons (45 ml) water. Place the chicken on top of everything. Reduce the heat to medium, cover, and cook until your cauliflower is tender and your chicken is cooked through, completely opaque and juices run clear, about 5 minutes.

6. Top the chicken with your homemade Pico de Gallo before serving.

thai vegetable curry

If you think every entree needs meat, I'm going to bet this curry will change your mind. The coconut milk and curry paste make it rich and flavorful, and the veggies make it so hearty, you won't even miss the meat! Serve as is or over steamed cauliflower rice.

PREP TIME 10 minutes
TOTAL TIME 30 minutes
MAKES 4 servings

2 tablespoons (28 ml) extra-virgin olive oil or avocado oil

1 red bell pepper, cut into strips

1 yellow or orange bell pepper, cut into strips

½ white or yellow onion, diced into ½-inch (1 cm) pieces

1½ teaspoons minced garlic

1 cup (133 g) peeled, diced sweet potato, ½-inch (1 cm) cubes

1 medium zucchini, halved and sliced into half-moons

1½ cups (355 ml) vegetable broth

1 cup (235 ml) canned unsweetened coconut milk

3 tablespoons (48 g) tomato paste

2 tablespoons (30 g) Thai red curry paste

½ teaspoon salt

Handful of fresh baby spinach leaves

1. Add the oil to a large skillet over medium-high heat. Once hot, add the bell peppers and onion. Sauté until the peppers have a bit of browning and the onion is tender, 3 to 4 minutes. Add the garlic and sauté so that the garlic is golden in color, another minute.

2. Add the sweet potato, zucchini, broth, coconut milk, tomato paste, curry paste, and salt. Reduce the heat to medium. Cover and simmer, stirring occasionally, until the sweet potatoes are tender, about 15 minutes.

3. Stir in the spinach. The leaves will begin to wilt immediately. Taste and add extra salt and pepper, if desired.

TIP

- Do you really want to add a protein to your curry? Simply stir in 1 cup (125 g) shredded or (140 g) chopped cooked chicken before everything simmers. This dish is fantastic with or without it!

garlic crushed red pepper chicken stir-fry

You just cannot go wrong with chicken and green beans. This stir-fry has some heat thanks to the crushed red pepper flakes, too. Feel free to swap out the chicken for boneless pork chops if that's what you have on hand.

PREP TIME 10 minutes
TOTAL TIME 25 minutes
MAKES 4 servings

1 tablespoon (15 ml) extra-virgin olive oil or avocado oil

2 pounds (900 g) boneless, skinless chicken breasts, cut into 1-inch (2.5 cm) pieces

1 teaspoon dried basil

½ teaspoon salt

½ teaspoon black pepper

3 tablespoons (45 ml) coconut aminos

1 tablespoon (15 g) ghee

1½ teaspoons minced garlic

½ teaspoon ground ginger

½ teaspoon crushed red pepper flakes (see Tip)

1 pound (455 g) fresh green beans, trimmed and cut into halves or thirds

Sesame seeds, for garnish

1. Add the oil to a large skillet over medium-high heat. Once hot, add the chicken. Sprinkle the basil, salt, and black pepper on top and stir. Brown on all sides, 3 to 4 minutes. The chicken doesn't need to be completely cooked through at this point.

2. When the chicken is browned, stir in the coconut aminos, ghee, garlic, ginger, and red pepper flakes. Add the green beans and stir again.

3. Lower the heat to medium to medium-low. Cover and simmer for 10 minutes, stirring frequently to scrape up the browned bits from the bottom of the pan. (Those are yummy!) The chicken should be cooked through, completely opaque and juices run clear, and the green beans should be softened but not totally wilted.

4. Sprinkle with the sesame seeds before serving.

TIP
- If you want to limit the spiciness in this dish, start with ¼ teaspoon red pepper flakes instead of the full ½ teaspoon this recipe calls for.

savory skillet chicken & veggies

These chicken thighs achieve golden-brown perfection before simmering in a savory sauce of chicken stock, balsamic vinegar, garlic, and bacon. Carrots and asparagus complete this dish to give you that veggie boost we are always looking for at dinnertime. Save time by using frozen pearl onions and choose thin asparagus, which will cook faster.

PREP TIME 5 minutes
TOTAL TIME 30 minutes
MAKES 6 servings

3 slices bacon (turkey or pork), diced

1 teaspoon minced garlic

6 boneless, skinless chicken thighs, 1½ to 2 pounds total (680 to 900 g)

1 tablespoon (15 ml) extra-virgin olive oil or avocado oil

½ teaspoon salt, plus more to taste

½ teaspoon black pepper, plus more to taste

2 cups (244 g) peeled, sliced carrots, ¼-inch (6 mm)-thick slices

6 ounces (170 g) frozen pearl onions (no need to thaw)

2 cups (475 ml) chicken stock

2 tablespoons (28 ml) balsamic vinegar

12 sprigs fresh thyme, leaves stripped and chopped

1 tablespoon (2 g) chopped fresh rosemary

1 cup (134 g) quartered asparagus stalks

1 tablespoon (9 g) arrowroot flour
1 tablespoon (15 ml) cold water

1. Add the bacon to a large skillet and cook over medium-high heat, stirring frequently, until the bacon starts to get crispy, 2 to 3 minutes. (If using turkey bacon, add 1 tablespoon [15 ml] oil to the skillet first to help crisp it up.) Add the garlic and sauté until the bacon is crispy and the garlic is golden brown, about 2 additional minutes. Remove the bacon and garlic to a plate and set aside.

2. Lay the chicken thighs out on paper towels and pat dry.

3. Add the oil to the skillet. Place the chicken thighs in the pan and liberally sprinkle with salt and black pepper on the side facing up. Brown the chicken, flip, and brown the other side, about 5 minutes total. The chicken does not need to be cooked through at this point, but you do want to get each side beautifully browned before moving on to the next step.

4. Add the carrots, onions, stock, balsamic vinegar, thyme, rosemary, ½ teaspoon salt, and ½ teaspoon black pepper to the skillet. Stir, cover, and simmer over medium to medium-high heat for 10 minutes.

5. Add the asparagus along with the reserved bacon and garlic. Cover and simmer until the carrots are tender and the chicken reaches a minimum internal temperature of 165°F (74°C), about 5 minutes.

6. To thicken the sauce, remove the chicken from the pan and turn off the heat. In a small jar, shake together the arrowroot flour and water. Pour the slurry into the skillet and stir. The sauce will begin to thicken immediately. Add your chicken back to the skillet. Taste and add extra salt or black pepper, if desired.

paleo pad thai

While my husband's favorite dish is the tuna poke bowl on page 101, this pad Thai is a very close second. The almond sauce is delightful, and the butternut squash noodles are surprisingly so much like regular noodles!

PREP TIME 10 minutes
TOTAL TIME 25 minutes
MAKES 4 servings

CHICKEN & VEGGIES
2 tablespoons (28 ml) extra-virgin olive oil, divided

1 red bell pepper, thinly sliced

2 teaspoons minced garlic

2 large eggs

1 pound (455 g) boneless, skinless chicken breasts, sliced into thin pieces

1 teaspoon salt

½ teaspoon black pepper

6 cups (about 20 ounces, or 560 g) butternut squash noodles (see Tip)

½ cup (50 g) chopped scallions

½ cup (70 g) chopped cashews

Handful of cilantro, chopped, for garnish

ALMOND SAUCE
¼ cup (65 g) almond or cashew butter

3 tablespoons (45 ml) coconut aminos

1 tablespoon (15 ml) rice vinegar

1 tablespoon (20 g) raw honey

1 teaspoon fresh lime juice

¼ teaspoon salt

1. Make the Chicken & Veggies: Add 1 tablespoon (15 ml) of the oil to a large skillet over medium-high heat. Once hot, add the bell pepper. Sauté until the peppers start to soften, 2 minutes. Add the garlic and sauté for another minute so that the garlic is golden in color. Remove from the pan and set aside (the peppers won't be completely tender yet).

2. Meanwhile, whisk the eggs in a small bowl.

3. Add the chicken to the skillet with the remaining 1 tablespoon (15 ml) oil. Sauté, stirring frequently, until the chicken is nicely browned, about 3 minutes. The chicken doesn't need to be fully cooked yet.

4. While the chicken is browning, make the Almond Sauce: In a bowl, stir together the nut butter, coconut aminos, vinegar, honey, lime juice, and salt.

5. Reduce the heat to medium. Pour the whisked eggs into the skillet and stir. The eggs will cook quickly. Add the salt and black pepper to everything.

6. Add the butternut squash noodles to the skillet. Pour in your Almond Sauce. Use tongs to stir so everything is coated. Cover and simmer until the chicken is cooked through, and the noodles are tender, about 5 minutes.

7. Top with the scallions, cashews, and cilantro before serving.

TIP
- If you want to try a different veggie noodle, sweet potato noodles will cook in just about the same amount of time. Thick-cut zoodles would also work, but they'll get tender very quickly, so keep an eye on them as they simmer and don't leave them in the skillet long.

beef burrito bowl

Imagine a really spectacular burrito. Now, dump all those glorious ingredients into a bowl. Top with the most incredible, creamy avocado dressing and homemade pico de gallo ever, and *voilà*! A beef burrito bowl that contains everything you love (but is sneakily healthy)!

PREP TIME 15 minutes
TOTAL TIME 30 minutes
MAKES 4 servings

VEGGIES
2 tablespoons (28 ml)
extra-virgin olive oil

2 bell peppers of any color,
sliced into strips

1 white or yellow onion,
sliced into strips

PICO DE GALLO
1 medium tomato, diced
into ½-inch (1 cm) or
smaller pieces

½ any color onion, diced
into ½-inch (1 cm) or
smaller pieces

¼ to ½ small jalapeño,
seeded and diced (optional)

Handful of cilantro, chopped

Lime juice, to taste

Salt, to taste

GROUND BEEF
1 pound (455 g) 93% lean
ground beef or turkey

1 teaspoon chili powder

½ teaspoon garlic powder

½ teaspoon onion powder

½ teaspoon dried oregano

¼ teaspoon paprika

¼ teaspoon ground cumin

¼ teaspoon salt

CAULIFLOWER RICE
2 tablespoons (28 ml) extra-virgin olive oil

4 cups (16 ounces, or 455 g) fresh or frozen cauliflower rice

2 teaspoons fresh lime juice

½ teaspoon salt

¼ teaspoon chili powder

CREAMY AVOCADO DRESSING
1 avocado

Handful of cilantro

¼ teaspoon garlic powder

¼ teaspoon salt

1 cup (47 g) chopped
romaine lettuce

1. Make the Veggies: Heat the oil in a large skillet over medium-high heat. Add the bell peppers and onion. Sauté, stirring occasionally, until the peppers have a bit of browning and the onion is translucent, 3 to 4 minutes.

2. Meanwhile, make the Pico de Gallo. In a small bowl, stir together the tomato, onion, jalapeño (if using), and cilantro. Add the lime juice and salt a little at a time. Taste and add more until you get it how you like it. Set aside.

3. Remove the peppers and onion from the skillet and set aside.

4. Make the Ground Beef: Add your ground beef or turkey to the skillet and return to medium-high heat. Crumble the meat using your spatula and sauté until browned and cooked through, about 5 minutes. Add the chili powder, garlic powder, onion powder, oregano, paprika, cumin, and salt. Stir until combined. Remove the meat from the skillet and reduce the heat to medium.

5. Make the Cauliflower Rice: Drizzle the oil into the skillet. Add the cauliflower rice, lime juice, salt, and chili powder. Stir, cover, and cook until the cauliflower is tender, about 5 minutes.

6. While the Cauliflower Rice is cooking, make the Creamy Avocado Dressing: Add the avocado, ¼ cup (60 ml) water, cilantro, garlic powder, and salt to a blender. Blend until smooth and thick. Add more water, a little at a time, if you'd prefer a thinner consistency.

7. Assemble all the ingredients in individual bowls, or, if you want to assemble everything in the skillet together, do it like this: When the Cauliflower Rice is done, turn off the heat. Spread it in an even layer in the bottom of your skillet. Layer the peppers and onions on top. Then, layer your ground beef or turkey, chopped romaine, and Pico de Gallo. Give it all a drizzle or dollop of Creamy Avocado Dressing, and you're ready to eat!

TIP

- I usually double the Creamy Avocado Dressing ingredients because we love avocado in my home. You really only want to make as much as you'll use right away, though, since avocado browns quickly. It's not something you'll want to save for later.

easy chicken green bean stir-fry

Anyone else think red cabbage is underrated? It's the most gorgeous shade of purple that brightens up any dish! This tasty stir-fry includes this stunning veggie along with green beans, chicken, and a fantastic sauce (but feel free to use green cabbage, if you prefer). Enjoy as is or serve over steamed cauliflower rice or roasted spaghetti squash.

PREP TIME 10 minutes
TOTAL TIME 25 minutes
MAKES 4 servings

2 tablespoons (28 ml) extra-virgin olive oil

1½ pounds (680 g) boneless, skinless chicken breasts, cut into 1-inch (2.5 cm) pieces

1 pound (455 g) fresh green beans, trimmed and halved

½ head red or green cabbage, sliced into thin strips

Salt and black pepper

½ cup (120 ml) coconut aminos (see Tip)

1 tablespoon (15 ml) rice vinegar or apple cider vinegar

1 tablespoon (10 g) minced garlic

¼ to ½ teaspoon crushed red pepper flakes

1. Add the oil to a large skillet over medium-high heat. Once hot, add the chicken to one half of the skillet. Add the green beans and cabbage to the other half. Generously sprinkle salt and black pepper over everything. Sauté, stirring occasionally to flip and separate the chicken that gets stuck together, 4 to 5 minutes. The chicken should be close to done with some color but will not be cooked through. The green beans and cabbage will have a bit of brown.

2. Add the coconut aminos, vinegar, garlic, and red pepper flakes. Stir everything together, reduce the heat to medium, and cover. Simmer until your green beans and cabbage are softened and the chicken is cooked through, completely opaque and juices run clear, 5 to 6 minutes.

3. Turn off the heat and uncover. Let sit for 2 minutes to cook off a bit of the sauce.

TIP

- If you're not serving this stir-fry over something, you may want to reduce the amount of coconut aminos so you have a bit less sauce. Go with ⅓ cup (80 ml), if that's your preference.

- You'll notice in the cooking instructions that I like to start with my chicken and veggies separated in the skillet. That makes it easier to flip the chicken and get some parts browned. I do stir the chicken in with the veggies before reducing the heat and covering, but not until I see some color on my chicken first.

orange ginger beef stir-fry

Steak, broccoli, and an orange ginger sauce—sounds pretty tantalizing, doesn't it? There's more good news because this meal is ready in less than 20 minutes! Enjoy as is or over steamed cauliflower rice for an even more satisfying meal.

PREP TIME 5 minutes
TOTAL TIME 20 minutes
MAKES 4 servings

STEAK & VEGGIES
1 tablespoon (15 ml) extra-virgin olive oil

1 red bell pepper, cut into strips

1 teaspoon minced garlic

1 pound (455 g) sirloin steak, cut into thin strips

1 pound (455 g) broccoli florets

½ teaspoon salt

½ teaspoon black pepper

ORANGE GINGER SAUCE
¼ cup (85 g) raw honey

2 tablespoons (28 ml) fresh orange juice

¼ teaspoon ground ginger

1. Make the Steak & Veggies: Add the oil to a skillet over medium-high heat. Once hot, add the bell pepper. Sauté until it has a bit of browning, 3 to 4 minutes. Add the garlic and sauté so that it is golden in color, another minute.

2. Add the steak and sauté so that all sides get a bit of crispy browning, 3 to 4 minutes. The beef doesn't need to be completely cooked through at this point.

3. Reduce the heat to medium. Stir in the broccoli, ¼ cup (60 ml) water, salt, and black pepper. Cover and let the broccoli steam until it's close to how you like it, usually 2 to 3 minutes to keep it bright with some crispness.

4. Meanwhile, make the Orange Ginger Sauce: Stir together the honey, orange juice, and ginger in a small bowl.

5. Pour the Orange Ginger Sauce over everything and stir. Reduce the heat to low and cover for 1 minute so the sauce is warm and the beef is cooked how you like it. Taste and add extra salt or black pepper, if desired.

chicken fried cauliflower rice

This dish has to be in my top-five most-made recipes list! It's the one that turns cauliflower rice skeptics into believers. Seriously. It looks and tastes so much like a classic chicken fried rice that it just keeps winning people over. This is one fast recipe I strongly suggest you try.

PREP TIME 10 minutes
TOTAL TIME 30 minutes
MAKES 4 servings

2 tablespoons (28 ml) extra-virgin olive oil or avocado oil

1½ pounds (680 g) boneless, skinless chicken breasts, cut into 1-inch (2.5 cm) pieces

½ white or yellow onion, diced into ½-inch (1 cm) pieces

1 cup (100 g) chopped green beans

½ cup (65 g) peeled, diced carrots, ½-inch (1 cm) dice

2 tablespoons (20 g) minced garlic

3 large eggs

1 head cauliflower, riced, or 3 to 4 cups (12 to 16 ounces, or 340 to 455 g) store-bought riced cauliflower (see Tip)

½ cup (120 ml) coconut aminos, plus more to taste

1 teaspoon salt

½ teaspoon garlic powder

½ teaspoon black pepper

¼ cup (25 g) chopped scallions, for garnish

1. Add the oil to a large skillet over medium-high heat. Once hot, add the chicken. Sauté, stirring frequently, until the chicken is nicely browned and cooked through, completely opaque and juices run clear, 4 to 5 minutes. Remove the chicken from the pan and set aside.

2. Reduce the heat to medium. To the same pan, add the onion. Cook until translucent, 3 to 4 minutes.

3. Add the green beans, carrots, and garlic. I like to leave the green beans and carrots a little crunchy, so I prefer to give them a quick sauté for about 3 minutes. You can cook them longer if you like them softer.

4. In a small bowl, whisk the eggs and then pour into the pan, stirring constantly. They'll cook quickly, in about 2 minutes.

5. Add the chicken back to the pan, along with the cauliflower rice, coconut aminos, salt, garlic powder, and black pepper and stir. Cover and steam until the rice is tender, 4 to 5 minutes.

6. Taste and add additional salt, black pepper, and coconut aminos as desired. Garnish with the scallions before serving.

TIP
- To create the cauliflower "rice," trim and chop the cauliflower into large chunks and place in a high-powered blender or food processor. Pulse until the cauliflower is a very small rice-like texture. You can use 3 to 4 cups (12 to 16 ounces, or 340 to 455 g) store-bought riced cauliflower to save time, if you prefer.

creamy buffalo chicken with zoodles

This creamy Buffalo sauce is dairy free but still incredibly thick. You'll be obsessed with using cashews for sauces after this recipe.

PREP TIME 15 minutes
+ cashew soak time
TOTAL TIME 25 minutes
MAKES 4 servings

CREAMY BUFFALO SAUCE
1 cup (140 g) raw cashews (see Tip)

1½ tablespoons (25 ml) extra-virgin olive oil

½ white onion, diced into ½-inch (1 cm) pieces

1 tablespoon (10 g) minced garlic

¼ cup (60 ml) hot sauce (see Tip)

1 tablespoon (4 g) nutritional yeast

1 teaspoon salt

½ teaspoon black pepper

CHICKEN
1 tablespoon (15 ml) extra-virgin olive oil or avocado oil

1 pound (455 g) boneless, skinless chicken breasts, cut into 1-inch (2.5 cm) pieces

½ teaspoon salt

ZOODLES
4 medium zucchini, or 20 ounces (560 g) store-bought zoodles (see Tip)

1. Make the Creamy Buffalo Sauce: Soak the cashews in water to cover for at least 1 hour. Drain the water when you're ready to cook.

2. Add the oil to a skillet over medium-high heat. Once hot, add the onion. Sauté until tender, 3 to 4 minutes. Add the garlic and sauté until it is golden, another minute.

3. Transfer to a high-powered blender or food processor, along with the soaked cashews, ¾ cup (175 ml) water, the hot sauce, nutritional yeast, salt, and black pepper. Blend until smooth. Taste and add more salt or hot sauce, if desired.

4. Make the Chicken: Add the oil to the skillet and return to medium-high heat. Add the chicken and sauté to brown all sides, about 3 minutes, using a spatula to separate the pieces when they get stuck together. Cook until the chicken is cooked through, completely opaque and juices run clear. Add the salt.

5. Meanwhile, prepare your Zoodles: Make zucchini noodles from the zucchini using a spiralizer according to the manufacturer's directions.

6. Reduce the heat to medium-low. Pour the Creamy Buffalo Sauce into the skillet with the chicken. Use tongs to stir in the zoodles. Cover and simmer until the zoodles are how you like them. This can take as little as 2 minutes, if you're using the thin store-bought zoodles, or as long as 5 minutes, if you make your own thick zoodles (my preference).

TIP
- To soften cashews quickly, add the cashews to a bowl, and water to cover, and microwave for about 1 minute.

- Look for a hot sauce with a simple ingredients list of cayenne red pepper, vinegar, salt, water, and garlic powder.

6

---

stovetop soups

There is nothing like a bowl of soup to warm you from the inside out. Unfortunately, so many soups call for you to slowly simmer until the end of time. I am of the opinion that it is possible to bring out tons of flavor without that eternal simmering, so the soups you'll find in this chapter are fast, my friend.

I've included options with meat as well as some that are vegan or vegetarian. Some have a thin broth and some are ridiculously thick and creamy. Take your pick! I know you'll find something you'll love!

Are you craving some heat? My Spicy Tomato Soup (page 144), Chicken Sausage Gumbo Soup (page 143), and Spicy Chipotle Chicken Chili (page 161) are sure to satisfy!

Does feeding little ones have you searching for new ideas? My kids love the Healthy 30-Minute Hamburger Soup (page 151) and Herby Lemon Chicken Soup (page 169).

Are you interested in incorporating some vegetarian options? Check out my Creamy Dairy Free Veggie Chowder (page 163) or my Ratatouille Soup (page 167). They're both rich and hearty without any dairy or meat.

no-bean 30-minute chili

This yummy chili is thick. It's hearty. It's dark. It doesn't have beans, but you're not going to notice. It's a chili you are going to want to make on a regular basis.

PREP TIME 5 minutes
TOTAL TIME 30 minutes
MAKES 6 to 8 servings

2 pounds (900 g) lean ground beef or turkey

1 green bell pepper, finely chopped

1 large yellow onion, finely chopped

2 cans (14.5 ounces, or 410 g, each) diced tomatoes

2 cups (475 ml) beef stock

1 can (6 ounces, or 170 g) tomato paste

¼ cup (40 g) minced garlic

1½ tablespoons (12 g) chili powder

1½ teaspoons paprika

1½ teaspoons onion powder

1½ teaspoons salt

1 teaspoon garlic powder

1 teaspoon ground cumin

1 teaspoon black pepper

Sliced scallions, diced onion, chopped avocado, or chopped cilantro, for garnish

1. Add the ground beef or turkey to a soup pot over medium-high heat. Use a spatula to crumble.

2. Add the bell pepper and onion. Cook, stirring occasionally, until the beef is browned and the veggies are softened, about 5 minutes.

3. Add the tomatoes, stock, tomato paste, garlic, chili powder, paprika, onion powder, salt, garlic powder, cumin, and black pepper. Stir. Reduce the heat to medium, cover, and simmer until the flavors marry, about 20 minutes.

4. Taste and add extra salt or black pepper, if you like. Serve with desired toppings.

TIP
- If your meat isn't very lean, you'll want to drain the grease after browning it. I use a 93% lean beef, so I don't drain mine.

beef stroganoff soup

This soup has all the flavor of a classic beef stroganoff, but it's oh so much lighter! It's rich, creamy, and tastes like it has been simmering for ages. I can't wait for you to try it!

PREP TIME 5 minutes
TOTAL TIME 30 minutes
MAKES 6 to 8 servings

1 tablespoon (15 ml) extra-virgin olive oil or ghee (For dairy-free dishes, use extra-virgin olive oil.)

1 pound (455 g) sirloin steak, sliced into small pieces

8 ounces (225 g) sliced mushrooms

½ white or yellow onion, diced into ½-inch (1 cm) pieces

2 teaspoons minced garlic

32 ounces (946 ml) beef stock

⅔ cup (160 ml) unsweetened, full-fat coconut milk, stirred

1 teaspoon balsamic vinegar

¾ teaspoon salt

½ teaspoon black pepper

½ teaspoon dried thyme

2 cups (8 ounces, or 225 g) cauliflower rice

1. Add the oil or ghee to your soup pot over medium-high heat. Once hot, add the steak, mushrooms, onion, and garlic. Sauté until the onion becomes tender and the steak is beautifully browned, about 5 minutes.

2. Add the stock, coconut milk, vinegar, salt, black pepper, and thyme. Cover, reduce the heat to medium, and simmer for 10 minutes.

3. Stir in the cauliflower rice. Cover and continue to simmer until the cauliflower is tender, another 10 minutes.

TIP
- The coconut milk helps create a creaminess in this soup that's reminiscent of traditional beef stroganoff. You will not taste any coconut in this dish since we're not using much, and I've paired it with plenty of other bold flavors that overpower it.

chicken sausage gumbo soup

I grew up in Mississippi, and our proximity to Louisiana meant gumbo was always available. My version of the New Orleans classic is a soup that's packed with chicken, okra, onion, bell pepper, celery, and lots of seasonings. It's a dish that's big on taste but ready in no time at all! I guarantee nobody will realize this is a healthy version!

PREP TIME 10 minutes
TOTAL TIME 30 minutes
MAKES 6 to 8 servings

2 tablespoons (28 ml) extra-virgin olive oil or ghee (For dairy-free dishes, use extra-virgin olive oil.)

1 white or yellow onion, diced into ½-inch (1 cm) pieces

1 cup (120 g) diced celery, ½-inch (1 cm) dice

1 green bell pepper, diced into ½-inch (1 cm) pieces

1 tablespoon (10 g) minced garlic

32 ounces (946 ml) chicken stock

1 pound (455 g) boneless, skinless chicken breasts, cut into 1-inch (2.5 cm) pieces

1 can (14.5 ounces, or 410 g) diced tomatoes

½ pound (225 g) okra, sliced into 1-inch (2.5 cm) pieces

2 precooked chicken sausages, sliced

1 bay leaf

½ teaspoon dried thyme

½ teaspoon dried basil

½ teaspoon salt

½ teaspoon black pepper

¼ teaspoon cayenne pepper

3 cups (12 ounces, or 340 g) fresh or frozen cauliflower rice

1. Add the oil or ghee to your soup pot over medium-high heat. Once hot, add the onion, celery, bell pepper, and garlic. Sauté until the onion becomes tender and fragrant, 3 to 4 minutes.

2. Add the stock, chicken, tomatoes, okra, sausages, bay leaf, thyme, basil, salt, black pepper, and cayenne pepper. Bring to a boil over high heat. Cover, reduce the heat to medium, and simmer for 10 minutes.

3. Stir in the cauliflower rice. Cover and continue to simmer until the cauliflower is tender and the chicken cooked through, another 8 to 10 minutes. Remove the bay leaf before serving.

spicy tomato soup

This isn't the tomato soup of your childhood. At least it's not mine, which was from a can and inspired a standoff between me and my parents. This effortless soup is made from fresh tomatoes—no need to even chop them!—and has a kick, thanks to jalapeños.

PREP TIME 5 minutes
TOTAL TIME 30 minutes
MAKES 6 to 8 servings

2 tablespoons (28 ml) extra-virgin olive oil or ghee (For vegan dishes, use extra-virgin olive oil.)

1 white or yellow onion, coarsely chopped

1 tablespoon (10 g) minced garlic

32 ounces (946 ml) chicken or vegetable stock (For vegan and vegetarian dishes, use vegetable stock.)

3 pounds (1.4 kg) fresh tomatoes (see Tip)

1 or 2 jalapeños, ribs and seeds removed

¼ cup (64 g) tomato paste

1 teaspoon salt

1 teaspoon black pepper

1 teaspoon garlic powder

½ teaspoon ground cumin

Chopped fresh herbs, for garnish

1. Add the oil or ghee and onion to your soup pot. Sauté on medium-high heat until the onion softens and becomes a bit translucent, 3 to 5 minutes. Add the garlic and sauté for another minute until the garlic is golden in color.

2. Add the stock, tomatoes, and jalapeños. Cover and cook until the tomato skins wrinkle and pull back from the tomato flesh, 10 to 15 minutes.

3. Transfer the mixture to a high-powered blender, along with the tomato paste, salt, black pepper, garlic powder, and cumin. Blend, in batches, if necessary, until smooth. Alternatively, you can use an immersion blender to purée the mixture right in the soup pot.

4. If using a high-powered blender, pour the soup back into your pot to warm through. Ladle the soup into bowls and garnish with fresh herbs to really impress your guests.

TIP
- Use any tomatoes you like. I've used beefsteak, Roma, and a combo of both with some cherry tomatoes thrown in to hit the 3-pound (1.4 kg) mark.

chicken curry soup

Craving all the flavor of curry but want it fast? This soup features a creamy curry broth, chicken, bell peppers, and sweet potato. It's a simple dish that packs tons of flavor.

PREP TIME 10 minutes
TOTAL TIME 30 minutes
MAKES 6 to 8 servings

2 tablespoons (28 ml) extra-virgin olive oil or avocado oil

2 red bell peppers, diced into ½-inch (1 cm) pieces

1 white or yellow onion, diced into ½-inch (1 cm) pieces

1 teaspoon minced garlic

1½ pounds (680 g) boneless, skinless chicken breasts, cut into 1-inch (2.5 cm) pieces

2 cups (266 g) diced sweet potatoes, 1-inch (2.5 cm) cubes

32 ounces (946 ml) chicken stock

1 can (14.5 ounces, or 410 g) diced tomatoes

¼ cup (64 g) tomato paste

1 tablespoon (6 g) curry powder

1 teaspoon ground ginger

1 teaspoon salt

½ teaspoon cayenne pepper

¼ teaspoon ground cumin

¼ teaspoon coriander

1 can (13.5 ounces, or 380 g) unsweetened full-fat coconut milk

Fresh cilantro, chopped

1. Add the oil to your soup pot over medium-high heat. Once hot, add the bell peppers and onion. Sauté until the onion is tender, 3 to 5 minutes. Add the garlic and sauté for another minute so the garlic is golden in color.

2. Add the chicken, sweet potatoes, stock, tomatoes, tomato paste, curry powder, ginger, salt, cayenne pepper, cumin, and coriander. Bring to a boil over high heat. Cover and reduce the heat to medium. Simmer until the chicken is cooked through and the sweet potato is tender, 15 to 20 minutes.

3. Remove from the heat and stir in the coconut milk. Top with fresh chopped cilantro when you're ready to serve!

beef "barley" soup

Is there barley in here? No, it's cauliflower rice! It's a perfect swap because it really looks so much like barley and absorbs whatever flavors you cook it with. Steak, veggies, and a tasty broth make this soup a complete meal.

PREP TIME 5 minutes
TOTAL TIME 30 minutes
MAKES 6 to 8 servings

1½ tablespoons (25 ml) extra-virgin olive oil or ghee (For dairy-free dishes, use extra-virgin olive oil.)

1 to 1½ pounds (455 to 680 g) sirloin steak, sliced into small pieces

½ white or yellow onion, diced into ½-inch (1 cm) pieces

1 cup (120 g) diced celery, ½-inch (1 cm) dice

1 cup (70 g) sliced mushrooms

1 cup (122 g) peeled, sliced carrots, ¼-inch (6 mm)-thick slices

1 tablespoon (10 g) minced garlic

32 ounces (946 ml) beef stock

2 tablespoons (32 g) tomato paste

2 tablespoons (28 ml) balsamic vinegar

2 teaspoons salt

1½ teaspoons black pepper

1 teaspoon dried thyme

1 teaspoon dried rosemary

1 teaspoon dried oregano

3 cups (12 ounces, or 340 g) fresh or frozen cauliflower rice

1. Add the oil or ghee and steak to your soup pot over medium-high heat. Brown all sides of the steak pieces, 3 to 4 minutes. Remove from the pot and set aside.

2. Add the onion, celery, mushrooms, carrots, and garlic to the pot. You should have enough fat from the beef already remaining, but add another 1½ teaspoons oil if not. Sauté until the onion becomes tender and fragrant, about 4 minutes.

3. Add the steak back to the pot along with the stock, tomato paste, vinegar, salt, black pepper, thyme, rosemary, and oregano. Reduce the heat to medium, cover, and simmer for 10 minutes.

4. Stir in the cauliflower rice. Cover and simmer until the cauliflower is soft, 8 to 10 minutes.

easiest vegetable soup

A truly delicious homemade vegetable soup doesn't need any meat at all. Mine is full of fresh veggies, including green beans, carrots, and sweet potatoes. They're swimming in a rich broth that will keep you coming back for more.

PREP TIME 10 minutes
TOTAL TIME 30 minutes
MAKES 6 to 8 servings

1 tablespoon (15 ml) extra-virgin olive oil or avocado oil

½ large white or yellow onion, diced into ½-inch (1 cm) pieces

1 teaspoon minced garlic

32 ounces (946 ml) chicken or vegetable stock (For vegan and vegetarian dishes, use vegetable stock.)

1 can (14.5 ounces, or 410 g) diced tomatoes

1 cup (100 g) chopped green beans

1 cup (122 g) peeled, sliced carrots, ¼-inch (6 mm)-thick slices

1 cup (133 g) diced sweet potatoes, ½-inch (1 cm) cubes

½ teaspoon salt

½ teaspoon black pepper

1 packed cup (about half a 5-ounce, or 140 g, package) baby spinach

¼ cup (15 g) chopped fresh parsley

1. Add the oil to your soup pot over medium to medium-high heat. Once the oil is hot, add the onion and sauté until softened, 3 to 4 minutes. Add the garlic and sauté for another minute so the garlic is golden in color.

2. Add the stock, tomatoes, green beans, carrots, sweet potatoes, salt, and black pepper. Bring to a boil over high heat. Cover, reduce the heat to medium, and simmer until the veggies are tender, 15 to 20 minutes.

3. Stir in the spinach and parsley. They will wilt right away. Taste and add extra salt or black pepper, if desired.

creamy seafood bisque

This creamy seafood bisque is one of my husband's favorites, and if you're a seafood lover, it's sure to be high on your list too! It looks and tastes like it's full of cream, but it's not. Instead, we use blended cauliflower and coconut milk to re-create that creaminess we associate with an amazing bisque. Use whatever seafood you like (I use a mixture of cod and shrimp) and adjust the hot sauce to your liking.

PREP TIME 10 minutes
TOTAL TIME 25 minutes
MAKES 6 servings

2 tablespoons (28 g) ghee or (28 ml) extra-virgin olive oil (For dairy-free dishes, use extra-virgin olive oil.)

3 cups (12 ounces, or 340 g) fresh or frozen cauliflower rice

½ white or yellow onion, coarsely chopped

2 ribs celery, chopped (about ¾ cup, or 75 g)

1 tablespoon (10 g) minced garlic

3 cups (700 ml) chicken or vegetable stock

1 cup (235 ml) canned unsweetened full-fat coconut milk, stirred

1½ teaspoons hot sauce (see Tip)

1½ teaspoons salt

1 teaspoon Old Bay seasoning

1 teaspoon dried thyme

1 to 1½ pounds (455 to 680 g) seafood

1. Add the ghee or oil to a soup pot over medium-high heat. Once hot, add the cauliflower rice, onion, celery, and garlic. Cover and cook, stirring occasionally, until the cauliflower and onion are tender, 6 to 8 minutes.

2. Transfer the mixture to a high-powered blender along with the stock and coconut milk. Blend until smooth. Alternatively, you can use an immersion blender to purée the mixture right in the soup pot.

3. If using a high-powered blender, pour the blended soup back into your pot. Add the hot sauce, salt, Old Bay, and thyme. Bring to a simmer over medium heat. Stir in your seafood and simmer until cooked through, 3 to 4 minutes.

TIP
- This soup has a little heat, so reduce the amount of hot sauce you use if that's your preference.

chicken zoodle soup

This chicken zoodle soup feels exactly like a traditional chicken noodle soup, even though there's nary a noodle in there. Think about it. When you're eating chicken noodle soup, you're not tasting the noodles, are you? Nope! It's all about that broth, tender vegetables, and chunks of chicken. This soup gives you all of that and still remains very light! It's perfect for a chilly evening at home.

PREP TIME 10 minutes
TOTAL TIME 30 minutes
MAKES 8 to 10 servings

1½ tablespoons (25 ml) extra-virgin olive oil or avocado oil

5 large carrots, peeled and chopped into ½-inch (1 cm) pieces

3 ribs celery, diced into ½-inch (1 cm) pieces

1 medium white or yellow onion, diced into ½-inch (1 cm) pieces

1 tablespoon (10 g) minced garlic

64 ounces (1.9 L) chicken stock

3 pounds (1.4 kg) boneless, skinless chicken breasts, cut into 1-inch (2.5 cm) pieces

¾ teaspoon salt

½ teaspoon black pepper

½ teaspoon garlic powder

4 to 6 medium zucchini, or 20 ounces (560 g) store-bought zoodles (see Tip)

½ cup (8 g) chopped fresh cilantro or (30 g) parsley

1. Add the oil to a soup pot over medium-high heat. Once hot, add the carrots, celery, onion, and garlic. Sauté until the onion is tender, stirring occasionally, about 5 minutes. (The carrots do not need to be completely cooked through at this point.)

2. Add the stock, chicken, salt, black pepper, and garlic powder. Bring to a simmer. Reduce the heat to medium, cover, and cook until the chicken is cooked through, completely opaque and juices run clear, 15 to 20 minutes.

3. While the soup is simmering, prepare the zoodles. Make zucchini noodles from the zucchini using a spiralizer according to the manufacturer's directions.

4. Add your zoodles to the pot along with your chopped cilantro or parsley. Stir and remove the pot from the heat. The zoodles will cook quickly just from sitting in the hot soup. Taste and add extra salt and black pepper, if desired.

TIP

- You absolutely can use 20 ounces (560 g) of store-bought zoodles; however, they tend to be very thin and fall apart quickly. Spiralizing your own noodles means you can get them nice and thick so they hold up well in a soup.

- If you're planning to meal prep with this recipe, leave the zoodles out and incorporate them only when you're ready to eat. Reheated zoodles can get too soft because they contain so much water. Let everything else simmer (even the fresh herbs), freeze or refrigerate, and then add the zoodles when it's time to chow down!

healthy 30-minute hamburger soup

I feel like most people grew up eating hamburger soup, but for some reason, I didn't discover it until adulthood. And I do love it! My version is made with only wholesome ingredients and is ready in about 25 minutes. In order to cook your soup quickly and avoid it being too much like a stew, cut your potatoes and other veggies into ½-inch (1 cm) pieces. This means you'll also get a little of everything in every bite!

PREP TIME 10 minutes
TOTAL TIME 30 minutes
MAKES 8 to 10 servings

1 pound (455 g) 93% lean ground beef

½ white or yellow onion, diced into ½-inch (1 cm) pieces

1 tablespoon (10 g) minced garlic

32 ounces (946 ml) beef stock

2 medium white sweet potatoes, peeled and cut into 1-inch (2.5 cm) cubes (see Tip)

2 medium carrots, peeled and cut into half circles ¼ inch (6 mm) thick

1 cup (100 g) chopped green beans

1 can (14.5 ounces, or 410 g) diced tomatoes

2 tablespoons (32 g) tomato paste

1 teaspoon dried thyme

1 teaspoon dried oregano

1 teaspoon salt

1 teaspoon onion powder

½ teaspoon black pepper

¼ cup (15 g) chopped fresh parsley

1. Add the ground beef and onion to a soup pot over medium-high heat. Use a spatula to crumble your beef and sauté until browned, stirring occasionally, about 5 minutes. Add the garlic and sauté for another minute so the garlic is golden in color.

2. Add the stock, sweet potatoes, carrots, green beans, tomatoes, tomato paste, thyme, oregano, salt, onion powder, and black pepper. Cover, reduce the heat to medium, and simmer until the veggies are tender, 15 to 20 minutes. Taste and add extra salt or black pepper, if desired. Ladle into bowls and top with fresh chopped parsley.

TIP
- I'm using white sweet potatoes here because they have a drier texture than their orange counterparts, so they better resemble a russet. You can, of course, use any potato you like!

quick stuffed-pepper soup

This soup has everything you love about stuffed peppers in one bowl—ground beef, onion, bell peppers, tomatoes, rice (it's cauliflower!), and plenty of seasoning!

PREP TIME 10 minutes
TOTAL TIME 30 minutes
MAKES 6 to 8 servings

1 pound (455 g) 93% lean ground beef

2 bell peppers of any color, diced into ½-inch (1 cm) pieces

1 white or yellow onion, diced into ½-inch (1 cm) pieces

1 tablespoon (10 g) minced garlic

32 ounces (946 ml) beef stock

¼ cup (64 g) tomato paste

2 teaspoons Italian seasoning

1 teaspoon salt

½ teaspoon garlic powder

½ teaspoon onion powder

½ teaspoon black pepper

2 cups (8 ounces, or 225 g) fresh or frozen cauliflower rice

1. Add your ground beef to a soup pot over medium-high heat. Use your spatula to crumble. Add in the bell peppers and onion. Cook, stirring occasionally, until the beef is browned. Add the garlic and sauté for another minute so the garlic is golden in color. (If your beef isn't giving you enough fat for sautéing the peppers and onion, add 1 tablespoon [15 ml] oil.)

2. Add the stock, tomato paste, Italian seasoning, salt, garlic powder, onion powder, and black pepper. Stir, cover, reduce the heat to medium, and simmer for 10 minutes.

3. Stir in the cauliflower rice. Cover and simmer until the cauliflower is soft, another 5 to 10 minutes. Taste and add extra salt or black pepper if you like.

hearty barbecue chicken soup

This thick soup has a flavor that is reminiscent of a lightly sweetened honey-barbecue sauce. It's a surprising twist on chicken soup! And, it's ready in about 20 minutes because we start with cooked shredded chicken (use leftover chicken or buy a rotisserie chicken!).

PREP TIME 5 minutes
TOTAL TIME 20 minutes
MAKES 6 servings

1 tablespoon (15 ml) extra-virgin olive oil or avocado oil

½ white or yellow onion, diced into ½-inch (1 cm) pieces

1 teaspoon minced garlic

2 cups (475 ml) chicken stock

2 cups (250 g) shredded cooked chicken

1 can (14.5 ounces, or 410 g) fire-roasted diced tomatoes

1 can (6 ounces, or 170 g) tomato paste

3 to 4 tablespoons (60 to 85 g) raw honey

1 teaspoon chili powder

½ teaspoon paprika

½ teaspoon salt

½ teaspoon black pepper

1. Add the oil to your soup pot over medium-high heat. Once hot, add the onion and sauté until tender with some browning, about 3 minutes. When the onion is almost done, stir in the garlic. Sauté for about 1 minute so that it has a bit of a golden color.

2. Add the stock, chicken, tomatoes, tomato paste, 3 tablespoons (60 g) honey, chili powder, paprika, salt, and black pepper. Stir, reduce the heat to medium, cover, and simmer until heated through, about 10 minutes.

3. Taste. Add more honey if you want it sweeter or salt and black pepper if you want to amp up the savory flavor a bit.

chicken & "rice" soup

There are so many flavorful aromatics and fresh herbs in this lovely soup! Plus, the chicken cooks in the broth to give you a robust flavor that soothes the soul and fills the belly.

PREP TIME 5 minutes
TOTAL TIME 30 minutes
MAKES 6 to 8 servings

1 tablespoon (15 ml)
extra-virgin olive oil
or avocado oil

1 white or yellow onion, diced
into ½-inch (1 cm) pieces

3 ribs celery, diced into
½-inch (1 cm) pieces

8 ounces (225 g) mushrooms,
chopped

2 teaspoons minced garlic

32 ounces (946 ml)
chicken stock

1 pound (455 g) boneless,
skinless chicken breasts, cut
into 1-inch (2.5 cm) pieces

1½ teaspoons fresh
chopped rosemary

1½ teaspoons chopped
fresh dill

1½ teaspoons salt

½ teaspoon black pepper

2 cups (8 ounces, 225 g) fresh
or frozen cauliflower rice

1. Add the oil to a soup pot over medium-high heat. Once hot, add the onion, celery, and mushrooms. Sauté until the onion and mushrooms are tender, about 5 minutes. Add the garlic and sauté for another minute so the garlic is golden in color.

2. Add the stock, chicken, rosemary, dill, salt, and black pepper. Bring to a boil over high heat. Cover, reduce the heat to medium, and simmer for 10 minutes.

3. Stir in the cauliflower rice. Cover and simmer until the cauliflower is soft and the chicken is cooked through, completely opaque and juices run clear, another 10 minutes. Taste and add more salt and pepper, if desired.

creamy butternut squash soup

This butternut squash soup is velvety smooth and creamy—but without the cream!
The squash tastes like it's been roasted, but to keep things simple, we sauté it with carrots,
onion, and garlic. This easy step brings out all its scrumptious flavor in very little time.
If fall were a soup, it would be this one!

PREP TIME 10 minutes
TOTAL TIME 30 minutes
MAKES 6 servings

**4 tablespoons (60 ml)
extra-virgin olive oil or
avocado oil, divided**

**3 carrots, peeled and sliced,
¼-inch (6 mm)-thick slices**

**½ white or yellow onion, diced
into ½-inch (1 cm) pieces**

**1 tablespoon (10 g)
minced garlic**

**2 pounds (900 g) butternut
squash, peeled and cut into
1-inch (2.5 cm) cubes
(see Tip)**

**3 to 4 cups (700 to
946 ml) chicken or vegetable
stock (see Tip) (For vegan
and vegetarian dishes, use
vegetable stock.)**

¾ teaspoon salt

½ teaspoon ground cinnamon

½ teaspoon ground nutmeg

**Canned unsweetened
coconut milk, for garnish
(optional)**

1. Add 2 tablespoons (28 ml) of the oil to a large skillet over
medium-high heat. Once hot, add the carrots and onion.
Sauté until the carrots are tender, 6 to 8 minutes. Add the garlic
and sauté for another minute so the garlic is golden in color.
Transfer to a high-powered blender. Set aside.

2. Add the remaining 2 tablespoons (28 ml) oil to the skillet, along
with the butternut squash, and return to medium-high heat.
Cover and cook, stirring occasionally, until the squash is tender
and has some beautiful browning, about 10 minutes. Transfer to
the blender. Add the stock, salt, cinnamon, and nutmeg. Blend
until smooth. (You may need to work in batches, depending on
the size of your blender.)

3. Taste and add more salt, if desired. Pour or ladle into bowls
and top with a drizzle of coconut milk, if desired, to make it look
extra special.

TIP
- For a thick soup, use 3 cups (700 ml) stock. For a thinner soup,
  use 4 cups (946 ml).

- Cut the butternut squash into cubes ¾ to 1 inch (2 to 2.5 cm)
  big. Some grocery stores carry prechopped squash in this very
  size. It's a huge time-saver!

supreme pizza chili

Supreme pizza in a bowl? If it sounds strange, you're in for a surprise. Beef, onion, pepperoni, olives (yes, olives!), tomatoes, bell pepper, and mushrooms make this fun chili really taste like a supreme pizza!

PREP TIME 10 minutes

TOTAL TIME 30 minutes

MAKES 6 servings

1 pound (455 g) 93% lean ground beef

½ white or yellow onion, diced into ½-inch (1 cm) pieces

1 teaspoon minced garlic

3 cups (700 ml) beef stock

1 can (14.5 ounces, or 410 g) diced tomatoes

1 cup (138 g) finely diced pepperoni (see Tip)

1 cup (70 g) sliced mushrooms

½ green bell pepper, diced into ½-inch (1 cm) pieces

3 tablespoons (48 g) tomato paste

2 tablespoons (12 g) Italian seasoning

1½ tablespoons (9 g) chopped black olives

1 teaspoon salt

½ teaspoon black pepper

1. Add your ground beef to a soup pot over medium-high heat. Use your spatula to crumble and add in the onion. Cook, stirring occasionally, until the beef is browned. Add the garlic and sauté for another minute so the garlic is golden in color. (If your beef isn't giving you enough fat to sauté the onion, add 1 tablespoon [15 ml] oil.)

2. Add the stock, tomatoes, pepperoni, mushrooms, bell pepper, tomato paste, Italian seasoning, olives, salt, and black pepper. Stir, cover, reduce the heat to medium, and simmer until the peppers are tender and the flavors have married, 15 to 20 minutes. Taste and add extra salt or black pepper if you like.

TIP
- Check the ingredients in your pepperoni! The one I prefer is actually made of turkey instead of pork and can be found in the natural foods section of higher-end grocery stores or in natural foods stores.

steak fajita stew

This hearty stew features the traditional flavors found in steak fajitas, including tender sirloin steak, peppers, onions, and fresh cilantro. Chunks of sweet potato make this dish extra satisfying too!

PREP TIME 10 minutes
TOTAL TIME 30 minutes
MAKES 6 servings

2 tablespoons (28 ml) extra-virgin olive oil or avocado oil

1½ pounds (680 g) sirloin steak, sliced into small pieces (see Tip)

1 white or yellow onion, diced into ½-inch (1 cm) pieces

1 green bell pepper, diced into ½-inch (1 cm) pieces

1 red bell pepper, diced into ½-inch (1 cm) pieces

1½ teaspoons minced garlic

3 cups (700 ml) beef stock

1 cup (133 g) diced sweet potatoes, 1-inch (2.5 cm) cubes

3 tablespoons (48 g) tomato paste

2 teaspoons chili powder

1 teaspoon salt

½ teaspoon onion powder

½ teaspoon garlic powder

½ teaspoon dried oregano

¼ teaspoon ground cumin

¼ cup (4 g) chopped fresh cilantro

1. Add the oil to your soup pot over medium-high heat. Add the steak and brown all sides of the steak pieces, 2 to 3 minutes. Remove from the pot and set aside.

2. Add the onion, bell peppers, and garlic to the pot. You should have enough fat from the beef already remaining, but you can add another 1½ teaspoons oil if necessary. Sauté until the onion becomes tender and fragrant, 3 to 4 minutes.

3. Add the steak back to the pot along with the sweet potatoes, tomato paste, chili powder, salt, onion powder, garlic powder, oregano, and cumin. Reduce the heat to medium, cover, and simmer until the sweet potato is softened, about 15 minutes.

4. Top with fresh cilantro when ready to serve!

TIP
• To keep this stew feeling like a true stew I use sirloin steak, but you absolutely can use a lean ground beef if you like. Both options are delicious in here!

spicy chipotle chicken chili

This is not a mild chili. Oh no, this one has some spiciness that really sets it apart!

PREP TIME 5 minutes
TOTAL TIME 30 minutes
MAKES 6 to 8 servings

1½ tablespoons (25 ml)
extra-virgin olive oil
or avocado oil

2 red bell peppers, diced into
½-inch (1 cm) pieces

1 white or yellow onion, diced
into ½-inch (1 cm) pieces

2 teaspoons minced garlic

2 cups (475 ml) chicken stock

1¾ to 2 pounds (795 to
900 g) boneless, skinless
chicken breasts, cut into
1-inch (2.5 cm) pieces
(see Tip)

1 can (28 ounces, or 785 g)
diced tomatoes

1 can (6 ounces, or 170 g)
tomato paste

1½ tablespoons (11 g)
chili powder

1½ teaspoons paprika

1 teaspoon chipotle
chili powder

1 teaspoon salt

1 teaspoon black pepper

¾ teaspoon ground cumin

½ teaspoon onion powder

½ teaspoon garlic powder

1. Add the oil to your soup pot over medium-high heat. Add the bell peppers and onion. Sauté until tender with some browning, 3 to 5 minutes. Add the garlic and let everything sauté for about another minute until the garlic turns a golden color.

2. Add the stock, chicken, tomatoes, tomato paste, chili powder, paprika, chipotle powder, salt, black pepper, cumin, onion powder, and garlic powder. Bring to a boil over high heat. Cover, reduce the heat to medium-high or medium, and simmer until the chicken is cooked through, completely opaque and juices run clear, about 15 minutes.

3. Taste and add extra salt or black pepper if you like.

TIP
- If you have a bit more time, keep the chicken breasts whole and simmer until cooked through to a minimum internal temperature of 165°F (74°C), 20 to 25 minutes. Remove to a cutting board, use two forks to shred, and mix back into the chili. I like having shredded chicken in my chili, so I prefer to do it this way when time permits.

creamy dairy-free veggie chowder

This thick, smooth chowder gives you veggies, veggies, and more veggies. We blend cauliflower with all the best aromatics for a creamy soup base you will swear includes dairy (but doesn't). If you fantasize about vegetables, this is the soup you want!

PREP TIME 10 minutes
TOTAL TIME 30 minutes
MAKES 6 servings

4 tablespoons (60 ml) extra-virgin olive oil or avocado oil, divided

4 cups (16 ounces, or 455 g) cauliflower rice

½ white or yellow onion, coarsely chopped

1 tablespoon (10 g) minced garlic

2½ to 3 cups (570 to 700 ml) vegetable stock (see Tip)

½ cup (120 ml) unsweetened full-fat coconut milk, stirred

1 teaspoon salt

5 carrots, peeled and sliced ¼ inch (6 mm) thick (about 1½ cups, or 183 g)

5 ribs celery, chopped (about 1½ cups, or 150 g)

1 medium zucchini, halved and cut into half-moons (about 1½ cups, or 180 g)

½ bunch asparagus, trimmed and cut into thirds or fourths (about 2 cups, or 268 g)

1. Add 2 tablespoons (28 ml) of the oil to a soup pot over medium-high heat. Once hot, add the cauliflower rice, onion, and garlic. Cover and cook, stirring occasionally, until the cauliflower and onion are tender, 6 to 8 minutes. Transfer to a high-powered blender along with the stock, coconut milk, and salt. If using an immersion blender, transfer to a mixing bowl. Blend until smooth. Set aside.

2. Add the remaining 2 tablespoons (28 ml) oil to the pot. When hot, add the carrots, celery, zucchini, and asparagus. (If your asparagus has especially thin stalks, add them in the last 3 minutes of your cooking time instead of here.) Cover and sauté over medium-high (or medium) heat, stirring occasionally, until the carrots are tender, 6 to 8 minutes.

3. Pour the creamy soup back into the pot with the veggies. Stir and simmer for 2 to 3 minutes so everything is warm. Taste and add extra salt, if desired.

TIP
• For a thick soup, use 2½ cups (570 ml) vegetable stock. If you'd prefer a thinner consistency, use 3 cups (700 ml).

french onion soup

A rich French onion soup can take upwards of an hour to make. Allowing the onions and garlic to caramelize is really where all the magic happens. This is what creates that rich flavor we know and love! To keep the cook time short, I add a hit of flavor with balsamic vinegar; you won't believe it's done in 30 minutes. Enjoy this easy French onion soup as a meal or delicious side.

PREP TIME 10 minutes
TOTAL TIME 30 minutes
MAKES 6 to 8 servings

¼ cup (56 g) ghee or cooking fat of choice (For dairy-free dishes, do not use ghee.)

3 pounds (1.4 kg) yellow onions, sliced

2 tablespoons (20 g) minced garlic

6 cups (1.4 L) beef stock

3 to 4 tablespoons (45 to 60 ml) balsamic vinegar (see Tip)

2 bay leaves

1 teaspoon chopped fresh thyme

1 teaspoon salt

1 teaspoon black pepper

¼ teaspoon onion powder

¼ teaspoon garlic powder

1. Add the ghee to your soup pot over medium-high heat. Once hot, add the onions and garlic. Sauté, stirring frequently, until the onion is wilted with some browning, about 10 minutes. You can cover for the last minute to speed up the process.

2. Add the stock, 3 tablespoons (45 ml) of vinegar, bay leaves, thyme, salt, black pepper, onion powder, and garlic powder. Cover, reduce the heat to medium, and simmer until the onions are tender and the flavors marry, 10 to 15 minutes.

3. Taste and add extra salt, black pepper, or vinegar if you like. Remove the bay leaves before serving

TIP
- Balsamic vinegar is powerful, but it adds a sweetness I enjoy in place of wine in savory dishes. Start with 3 tablespoons (45 ml) and add another tablespoon (15 ml) after tasting, if desired.

ratatouille soup

Ratatouille is a French dish of stewed or roasted vegetables that takes a lot of time to prepare. We're switching things up and enjoying it as a soup to keep it fast but still a celebration of beautifully prepared fresh produce. Dice all your vegetables into ½-inch (1 cm) pieces so you'll have a bit of everything in each spoonful.

PREP TIME 15 minutes
TOTAL TIME 30 minutes
MAKES 6 to 8 servings

3 tablespoons (45 ml) extra-virgin olive oil or avocado oil, divided

1 red bell pepper, diced

1 yellow bell pepper, diced

1 white or yellow onion, diced

1 tablespoon (1 g) minced garlic

1 cup (82 g) diced eggplant

1 cup (120 g) diced yellow squash

1 cup (120 g) diced zucchini

32 ounces (946 ml) vegetable stock

2 cups (360 g) diced tomatoes

2 tablespoons (32 g) tomato paste

1 teaspoon salt

½ teaspoon black pepper

¼ teaspoon crushed red pepper flakes (optional)

2 tablespoons (8 g) chopped fresh parsley

1. Add 2 tablespoons (28 ml) of the oil to your soup pot over medium-high heat. Add the bell peppers and onion. Sauté until tender with some browning, 3 to 5 minutes. Add the garlic and sauté for about another minute until the garlic turns a golden color.

2. Add the eggplant, squash, and zucchini along with the remaining 1 tablespoon (15 ml) oil. Stir and give these veggies a quick sauté, about 2 minutes, just to bring out their flavors a bit more. We're not cooking them through here.

3. Add the stock, tomatoes, tomato paste, salt, black pepper, and red pepper flakes (if using). Cover, reduce the heat to medium, and simmer until the vegetables are tender, 10 to 15 minutes.

4. Stir in the chopped fresh parsley. Taste and add extra salt or black pepper if you like.

spicy sausage & cabbage soup

This spicy soup is inspired by my father's sausage and bean soup. Now hear me out, I know this has no beans in it. After one visit to my parents' house, I came home dreaming about the soup he kept serving up. It has layers upon layers of flavor and so much heat. I'll never get enough of the stuff. Of course, I immediately set out to re-create it in a Paleo-friendly way, and this incredible, spicy soup is the result.

PREP TIME 10 minutes
TOTAL TIME 30 minutes
MAKES 6 to 8 servings

2 tablespoons (28 ml)
extra-virgin olive oil
or avocado oil

1 pound (455 g) fully cooked
beef sausage, sliced into half
circles ¼ inch (6 mm) thick
(see Tip)

2 medium white or yellow
onions, diced into ½-inch
(1 cm) pieces

4 ribs celery, chopped

2 green bell peppers, diced
into ½-inch (1 cm) pieces

32 ounces (946 ml)
chicken stock

1 head cabbage, chopped

2 cans (28 ounces, or 785 g,
each) diced tomatoes

1 tablespoon plus
½ teaspoon Cajun or
Creole seasoning

Salt and black pepper,
to taste

4 scallions, sliced

½ cup (8 g) chopped
fresh cilantro

1. Add the oil to your soup pot over medium-high heat. Once hot, add the sausage, onion, and celery. Sauté until the sausage has some browning and the onion is tender, about 5 minutes. Add the bell peppers and sauté for an additional 3 minutes.

2. Add the stock, cabbage, tomatoes, and Cajun seasoning. If your sausage is already spicy, start with less seasoning and taste before adding more. Stir and bring to a boil. Reduce the heat to medium, cover, and simmer until the cabbage is tender and the flavors have married, 10 to 15 minutes.

3. Taste and add salt and black pepper. Stir in the scallions and cilantro a few minutes before you're ready to serve.

TIP
- Any full cooked sausage will work well here, so feel free to use chicken, pork, or turkey.

herby lemon chicken soup

A lemony broth and fresh herbs will have you coming back for more of this chicken soup. It's delightful any time of year!

PREP TIME 10 minutes
TOTAL TIME 30 minutes
MAKES 6 to 8 servings

1½ tablespoons (25 ml) extra-virgin olive oil or avocado oil

½ white or yellow onion, diced into ½-inch (1 cm) pieces

1 cup (120 g) diced celery, ½-inch (1 cm) dice

1 tablespoon (10 g) minced garlic

32 ounces (946 ml) chicken stock

1½ pounds (680 g) boneless, skinless chicken breasts or thighs, cut into 1-inch (2.5 cm) pieces (see Tip)

1 cup (130 g) peeled, diced carrots, ½-inch (1 cm) dice

1 cup (133 g) diced sweet potatoes, ½-inch (1 cm) cubes

3 tablespoons (45 ml) fresh lemon juice

1 tablespoon (4 g) chopped fresh dill

1 tablespoon (2 g) chopped fresh thyme

1½ teaspoons salt

1 teaspoon black pepper

¼ cup (15 g) chopped fresh parsley

1. Add the oil to your soup pot over medium-high heat. Once hot, add the onion and celery. Sauté until tender with some browning, 3 to 5 minutes. Add the garlic and sauté for about another minute until the garlic turns a golden color.

2. Add the stock, chicken, carrots, sweet potatoes, lemon juice, dill, thyme, salt, and black pepper. Bring to a boil over high heat. Cover, reduce the heat to medium, and simmer until the chicken is cooked through, completely opaque and juices run clear, and the sweet potatoes are tender, about 15 minutes.

3. Stir in the parsley. Taste and add extra salt or black pepper if you like.

TIP

- If you have a bit more time, keep the chicken breasts whole and simmer until cooked through to a minimum internal temperature of 165°F (74°C), 20 to 25 minutes. Remove to a cutting board, use two forks to shred, and mix back into the soup. I like having shredded chicken in my soup, so I prefer to do it this way when time permits.

7

swoonworthy one-dish desserts

I never tire of breakfast food. How about you? In fact, I believe breakfast shouldn't be limited to that first meal of the day. I'll whip up a hash or frittata for lunch or dinner when the craving hits!

Giving up or limiting refined sugar and white flour is not the end of the world, and it most certainly isn't the end of desserts. There are some incredible sweeteners and flours that make Paleo desserts possible! It's important to know up front that grain-free flours do not perform the same as the flour you're accustomed to. You cannot take a traditional cake recipe and swap white flour for a grain-free flour or sugar for honey and expect the same results. It won't work. While making Paleo desserts isn't hard, it definitely takes some finesse, some understanding of these ingredients, and sometimes, a little bit of extra time or preparation.

But don't worry. I'm going to make this shockingly easy because I've done all the necessary testing for you! The dessert recipes I'm sharing in this chapter are absolute favorites of mine. They're easy to make and plenty sweet. (I promise, I'm not going to try to convince you to call a handful of raisins "dessert.") You'll see that I like to use lots of fruit and coconut milk or cream to create healthy treats to satisfy your sweet tooth. And I can't wait for you to try my No-Fuss Fudgy Brownies (page 181)!

skillet blueberry almond cobbler

There's something about a cobbler with bubbling blueberries, orange, and almond. That flavor combo is divine, isn't it? Top it with coconut whipped cream for something special.

PREP TIME 10 minutes
TOTAL TIME 30 minutes
+ rest time
MAKES 8 servings

BLUEBERRY FILLING
**4 cups (580 g)
fresh blueberries**
⅓ cup (115 g) raw honey
Zest of 1 orange
**3 tablespoons (45 ml)
fresh orange juice**
2 teaspoons almond extract
⅛ teaspoon salt

CRUMBLE TOPPING
¾ cup (83 g) chopped pecans
¼ cup (28 g) almond flour
**¼ cup (60 g) unsweetened
applesauce**
**1 tablespoon (7 g)
coconut flour**
½ teaspoon almond extract
¼ teaspoon ground cinnamon
**2 tablespoons (28 ml)
unsweetened almond milk**

1. Preheat the oven to 450°F (230°C, or gas mark 8).

2. Make the Blueberry Filling: In a 10-inch (25.5 cm) cast-iron skillet, gently combine the blueberries, honey, zest, orange juice, almond extract, and salt. Spread in an even layer.

3. Make the Crumble Topping: Iin a large bowl, stir together the pecans, almond flour, applesauce, coconut flour, almond extract, and cinnamon. The final texture should be soft and clumpy.

4. Use your hands to scatter the crumble topping on top of the blueberry mixture. Gently press the topping down into your blueberries. The topping shouldn't be submerged; we just don't want it sitting completely on top of the blueberries. As it cooks, some of it will work its way down into your fruit filling.

5. Bake for 10 minutes. Remove from the oven and reduce the temperature to 425°F (220°C, or gas mark 7).

6. Drizzle the almond milk on top of the crumble. Bake in the oven and bake until the topping has some nice browning and the blueberries are bubbly, another 7 to 8 minutes.

7. After baking, let the cobbler sit for 15 minutes to set up. Serve warm or at room temperature.

MAKE COCONUT WHIPPED CREAM

Chill one can of coconut cream or coconut milk in the fridge overnight. (I recommend using canned coconut cream because it has less water.) Once chilled, scoop out the thick cream that separates to the top of the can. (Leave the liquid in the can. We won't use it for this recipe!) Whip using a stand mixer or handheld mixer for 2 to 3 minutes until soft peaks form. If you prefer your whipped cream a little sweeter, you can add a dash of vanilla and/or your sweetener of choice.

sautéed apples

I've been making these sautéed apples for my kids for years. It was one of the first desserts they ever enjoyed because the apples are soft and naturally sweetened with maple syrup. Sometimes, simple really is the best!

PREP TIME 10 minutes
TOTAL TIME 15 minutes
MAKES 4 servings

2 tablespoons (28 g) coconut oil or ghee (For dairy-free and vegan dishes, use coconut oil.)

4 cups (600 g) diced apples (unpeeled), ½-inch (1 cm) dice

1 tablespoon (15 ml) pure maple syrup (see Tip)

1 teaspoon ground cinnamon

½ teaspoon nutmeg

1. Add the oil or ghee to a nonstick skillet over medium-high heat until mostly melted.

2. Add the apples and sauté, stirring, occasionally, until softened, 5 to 8 minutes.

3. Once the apples are tender, stir in the maple syrup, cinnamon, and nutmeg. Serve warm or at room temperature.

TIP
- You're welcome to use additional maple syrup if you want these apples to be extra sweet!

chocolate mousse–stuffed strawberries

To create the chocolate mousse we're stuffing our strawberries with, refrigerate your coconut cream overnight. That will make it as firm as possible so that it doesn't become thin when blending. The finished mousse is lightly sweet and won't overpower your strawberries!

PREP TIME 20 minutes
+ overnight chill time
TOTAL TIME 20 minutes
MAKES 10 t0 12 servings

2 cans (13½ ounces, or 380 g, each) coconut cream (see Tip)

2 pounds (900 g) fresh large strawberries

2½ tablespoons (12.5 g) unsweetened cacao or cocoa powder

2 tablespoons (28 ml) pure maple syrup or (40 g) raw honey (For vegan dishes, use pure maple syrup.)

1. Chill the coconut cream in the refrigerator overnight. We're trying to encourage separation of the cream from the liquid.

2. Rinse the strawberries and pat dry. Remove the stems from the strawberries and then use a melon baller or small knife to scoop out a hole in the top of each.

3. If you want your strawberries to stand up, use a knife to cut a bit off the bottom of each strawberry so that it's flat and straight. Set aside while you make the chocolate mousse filling.

4. Carefully scoop out the solid coconut cream from the can and add it to a mixing bowl. Do not stir or shake the can. (Leave the liquid in the can for use in a smoothie or in a sauce later.)

5. Beat the hardened coconut cream with a mixer until creamy and smooth, 30 seconds. Check for lumps and make sure you smooth those out before moving to the next step. (Or just remove any stubborn clumps that refuse to cooperate.)

6. Add the cacao or cocoa powder and maple syrup or honey. Mix with a spatula or your beater until thoroughly combined.

7. To fill the strawberries, spoon the mousse into a resealable plastic bag with one corner cut off (or a piping bag if you're fancy). Pipe into each hollowed-out strawberry.

TIP

- Refrigerate any leftover mousse and use it as a fruit dip! It will continue to thicken in the fridge, so just give it a good stir before using.

- You can use coconut milk if you don't have coconut cream; however, you will not have as much solid cream in the can because the milk has a higher water content. This means you'll have less mousse. Start with 1½ tablespoons (25 ml) maple syrup and 1 tablespoon (5 g) cocoa powder

skillet apple cinnamon cobbler

This skillet cobbler is everything you'd want in an apple pie but much simpler to make and contains no refined sugar. I promise you, nobody will notice. Honey and applesauce make this dessert perfectly sweet! Top it with coconut whipped cream, if desired.

PREP TIME 10 minutes
TOTAL TIME 30 minutes
+ rest time
MAKES 8 servings

APPLE FILLING
6 cups (900 g) diced apples, ½-inch (1 cm) dice (unpeeled) (see Tip)

2 tablespoons (28 g) coconut oil

½ cup (170 g) raw honey

½ teaspoon ground cinnamon

¼ teaspoon ground nutmeg

CRUMBLE TOPPING
¾ cup (90 g) chopped walnuts, divided

¼ cup (28 g) almond flour

¼ cup (60 g) unsweetened applesauce

1 tablespoon (7 g) coconut flour

½ teaspoon vanilla extract

¼ teaspoon ground cinnamon

2 tablespoons (28 ml) unsweetened almond milk

1. Preheat the oven to 450°F (230°C, or gas mark 8).

2. Make the Apple Filling: Add the apples and oil to a 10-inch (25.5 cm) cast-iron skillet over medium-high heat. Sauté, stirring occasionally, until the apples are fairly soft, about 5 minutes. (To speed this up you can cover your skillet, but just be sure to uncover and let some of the excess liquid cook off before moving on to the next step.)

3. Meanwhile, make the Crumble Topping: In a large bowl, combine ½ cup (60 g) of the walnuts, almond flour, applesauce, coconut flour, vanilla, and cinnamon. The final texture should be clumpy.

4. Stir the honey, cinnamon, and nutmeg into the sautéed apples and remove from the heat.

5. Use your hands to scatter the crumble topping on top of the apple mixture. Gently press the topping down into your apples. The topping shouldn't be submerged in the filling; we just don't want it sitting completely on top of the apples. As it cooks, some of it will work its way down into your fruit filling.

6. Drizzle the almond milk over the topping and bake until bubbly and you have some browning on the crust, about 15 minutes.

7. Remove from the oven and sprinkle the remaining ¼ cup (30 g) walnuts on top. Let the cobbler sit for 15 minutes to set up. Serve warm or at room temperature.

> **TIP**
> • I recommend dicing your apples for this recipe, instead of using slices, as it speeds up the cooking process. And there's no need to peel those apples! The peel softens beautifully as it cooks.

dairy-free chocolate pudding

Oh, just wait until you try this decadent pudding! It is so sweet, creamy, and thick, it tastes like you're really indulging—but you can feel oh-so-good about these ingredients.

PREP TIME 5 minutes
TOTAL TIME 15 minutes
+ chill time
MAKES 4 servings

1 can (13½ ounces, or 380 g) coconut cream

½ cup (40 g) unsweetened cacao or cocoa powder

½ cup (120 ml) pure maple syrup or (170 g) raw honey (For vegan dishes, use pure maple syrup.)

½ teaspoon vanilla extract

3 tablespoons (27 g) arrowroot flour

3 tablespoons (45 ml) cold water

1. Add the coconut cream, cacao or cocoa powder, maple syrup or honey, and vanilla to a medium saucepan. Bring to a boil, whisking frequently. As soon as it begins to boil, remove from the heat.

2. Combine the arrowroot flour and water in a small jar. Shake until well combined. Pour the slurry into your warm pudding mixture, whisking so that the pudding is smooth and creamy. You'll notice the pudding has thickened but isn't quite as thick as you'll want it. Pour into a bowl, cover with plastic wrap, and place in the freezer for 1 hour to firm up.

TIP
- This pudding will keep in the refrigerator, covered, for up to 5 days, so it's ideal for meal prep!

sheet-pan blueberry granola

This Paleo granola is delicious for breakfast or snacking! It's loaded with nuts, pumpkin seeds, and dried blueberries. Plus, it's lightly sweetened with zero refined sugar. Bake and then store in an airtight container for up to 2 weeks of enjoyment.

PREP TIME 10 minutes
TOTAL TIME 30 minutes
+ cooling time
MAKES about 8 cups
(25 servings, ⅓ cup
[85 g] each)

2 cups (200 g) walnuts

2 cups (200 g) pecan halves

2 cups (220 g) slivered almonds

½ cup (70 g) pumpkin seeds

½ cup (120 ml) pure maple syrup or (170 g) raw honey (For vegan dishes, use pure maple syrup.)

3 tablespoons (45 g) coconut oil, melted

1 teaspoon ground cinnamon

2 cups (240 g) dried blueberries

1. Preheat the oven to 325°F (170°C, or gas mark 3) and set the oven rack to the middle position. Line a 12 x 17-inch (30 x 43 cm) baking sheet with parchment paper.

2. Coarsely chop the walnuts and pecans. You don't want them to be super small, but you don't want to have any giant pieces in there either. Spread in a single layer on the prepared baking sheet.

3. Scatter the almonds and pumpkin seeds on top.

4. In a small bowl, stir together the maple syrup or honey, oil, and cinnamon. Pour over your nut mixture and then use a spatula to stir it all together. You want everything thoroughly coated. Spread everything into an even layer.

5. Bake for 18 minutes and then turn the broiler to high. Broil (on the same middle baking rack) for 1½ to 2 minutes to achieve a light golden color. Watch your granola as it broils because it can quickly burn.

6. Remove from the oven and stir in the dried blueberries. Spread everything back into an even layer and let cool completely. The granola will get crispy as it cools.

7. Once completely cooled, store in an airtight container at room temperature. It will be good for at least 2 weeks, but I bet you'll have it all gobbled up long before then!

TIP
- Don't skimp on these blueberries! Make sure you select an unsweetened brand and use the full 2 cups (240 g). It's worth it because they really do add the perfect sweetness to each bite!

no-fuss fudgy brownies

So fudgy, dense, and perfectly soft, these brownies are made with Paleo baking flour, which is a premade blend of almond flour, coconut flour, and starches. For sweetness (because these are definitely sweet), we use coconut sugar and maple syrup. Want more good news? You don't need to break out your stand mixer. This dessert really is easy!

PREP TIME 5 minutes
TOTAL TIME 25 minutes
+ cooling time
MAKES 9 servings

1 cup (144 g) coconut sugar

½ cup (120 ml) pure
maple syrup

¼ cup (56 g) coconut oil,
melted

¼ cup (56 g) ghee, melted

2 large eggs

1½ teaspoons vanilla extract

¾ cups (69 g)
Paleo baking flour

¼ cup (20 g) unsweetened
cacao or cocoa powder

1. Preheat the oven to 400°F (200°C, or gas mark 6).
Line a 9 x 9-inch (23 x 23 cm) baking pan with parchment paper.

2. In a large bowl, stir together the coconut sugar, maple syrup, oil, and ghee until well combined.

3. Add the eggs and vanilla. Stir well.

4. Stir in the Paleo baking flour and cacao powder until well combined. Transfer the batter to the prepared pan.

5. Bake for 17 to 20 minutes or until a toothpick inserted into the center of the brownies comes out with crumbs. The toothpick should not be clean but it shouldn't be completely wet either. (You're going to be on the lower side of that time if using metal and on the higher side of that time if using glass or ceramic.)

6. After baking, cool until set, about 15 minutes, on the counter or a wire rack. Remove the brownies from the pan by lifting the edges of the parchment paper and slice into 9 squares.

TIP
- As a general rule, light-colored metal pans are favored for brownies because they cook evenly and prevent overbrowning. You can (and I have) use glass or ceramic, but be aware that this type of cooking vessel means your batter may need to cook a bit longer. Since it takes longer for the center to cook, it's also easier to burn the edge pieces, so keep a close eye on it.

easy fruit bake

Is this easy fruit bake a dessert or a beautiful addition to a brunch? It's both! You can even use it as a topping for biscuits, pancakes, or waffles! It's just so versatile and yummy.

PREP TIME 10 minutes
TOTAL TIME 30 minutes
MAKES 8 servings

32 ounces (900 kg)
frozen peach slices (see Tip)

2 cans (15 ounces, or 425 g,
each) pear halves in
100% juice, drained (see Tip)

2 tablespoons (28 g)
ghee, melted

1 teaspoon ground cinnamon

1 cup (100 g) fresh
cranberries

⅓ cup (80 ml) pure
maple syrup

1. Preheat the oven to 425°F (220°C, or gas mark 7).

2. Spread the frozen peaches in an even layer on the bottom of a 9 x 13-inch (23 x 33 cm) baking dish.

3. Add the pears on top of your peaches. Do not use the juice as this will give you too much liquid. (Why not incorporate that sweet juice in a smoothie instead? There's no sense wasting it!)

4. In a small bowl, combine the ghee and cinnamon. Pour over the peaches and pears.

5. Spread the cranberries on top and then drizzle the maple syrup over all the fruit.

6. Bake until the cranberries are bursting and the peaches have softened, about 20 minutes.

TIP
- Using canned pears and frozen peaches drastically cuts both our prep time (no chopping anything!) and baking time, so we can serve up this roasted fruit quickly. You can certainly use fresh fruit, if you prefer, but increase the baking time to somewhere closer to 45 minutes in order to give the fruit enough time to fully soften.

easy paleo chocolate muffins

These muffins are chocolaty and soft but made with simple Paleo ingredients! Cacao powder and your favorite dark chocolate bar work together to give us the rich flavor we crave in chocolate desserts. Plus, these muffins are incredibly easy to make. You can get the batter ready for the oven in as little as 5 minutes! How about that for a good-for-you sweet treat you can enjoy whenever the mood strikes?

PREP TIME 5 minutes
TOTAL TIME 25 minutes
+ rest time
MAKES 12 muffins

1 cup (112 g) almond flour

¼ cup (28 g) coconut flour

¼ cup (20 g) unsweetened cacao or cocoa powder

½ cup (72 g) coconut sugar

1 teaspoon baking soda

3 large eggs

1 cup (235 ml) almond milk

¼ cup (56 g) coconut oil, melted

1½ teaspoons vanilla extract

2½ ounces (70 g) Paleo dark chocolate bar, finely chopped (see Tip)

1. Preheat the oven to 375°F (190°C, or gas mark 5). Line a 12-cup muffin pan with liners.

2. In a large bowl, stir together the almond flour, coconut flour, cacao powder, coconut sugar, and baking soda until well combined.

3. Add the eggs, almond milk, oil, and vanilla. Stir well.

4. Fold in the chopped chocolate bar pieces.

5. Spoon the batter into the prepared muffin pan, dividing the batter evenly and filling each liner three-fourths of the way full.

6. Bake until a toothpick inserted into the center of the muffins comes out with crumbs, about 20 minutes. The toothpick should not be clean, but it shouldn't be completely wet either.

7. After baking, let the cupcakes cool briefly before enjoying.

TIP
- You're welcome to use your favorite Paleo chocolate bar in this recipe. The one I often select is 72% cacao and includes only cacao, coconut sugar, and cacao butter.

about the author

Christina Shoemaker is the creator of *The Whole Cook*, a popular food blog filled with hundreds of easy and good-for-you recipes. There she shares how to create flavorful meals the whole family will love using healthy ingredients. Most of her dishes are gluten free, dairy free, refined sugar free, macro friendly, and Paleo. All are delicious!

When not in her kitchen, Christina can usually be found reading fiction or trying to convince her two children that the living room is not where they should dump all their toys. It's an ongoing battle. She's losing.

acknowledgments

To all of my *The Whole Cook* readers, I cannot thank you enough for following along on this journey with me. I appreciate every kind comment and message you've sent, all of your encouragement, and your never-ending prodding to write a cookbook. I heard you! Look, I wrote a cookbook! I often refer to you as my friends and that's truly how I see you. I still cannot believe how far this little blog has come, and I sincerely thank you for trusting me with your meals. I made this cookbook for you.

To David, this cookbook would not be possible without you. You have listened to all my worries, fears, and outbursts of joy during this process. You believed in me and prodded me forward when I was overwhelmed. You ate reheated dinners (because I cook early in the day so the light will be best for photographs) with only minimal grumbling. You gave me the time and space to create this passion project, and I thank you so much for it. Also, a big thank you for the many occasions you let me escape to a coffee shop when I reached my breaking point. This cookbook wouldn't exist without you and caffeine.

To Wyatt and Maddie, I love you so incredibly much. Thank you for inspiring me to explore a healthier way of eating. Thank you for making me laugh daily. Thank you for all the hugs and kisses. Thank you for making me feel like the most special mom in all the world. I know God blessed me when He made me your mother, and I'm grateful every day for that privilege.

To my mom and dad, thank you for being my biggest cheerleaders all of my life. One of the greatest things you did as parents (and it's a very long list of great things) is make me feel that I could do anything I set my mind to. You always believed in me, and I aspire to show my own children that same encouragement.

To Jessie, my best friend and sister, thank you for talking me off the ledges. You're my favorite person to talk to about anything and everything. You always have the best ideas and insight. I love you so much.

To Vickey, the very best of all mother-in-laws. Thank you for flying to Arkansas and cooking with me for ten days as I was in the middle of my cookbook panic. Thank you for washing dishes, bouncing ideas around with me, and being such a fun cooking partner. I am so fortunate to call you family and love all of our time together!

To my Grandma Bessie, thank you for creating such fun childhood memories of being with you in the kitchen. Thank you for rushing out to buy shrimp that one Christmas Eve years ago when it's all I wanted and then using a blow dryer to thaw them when you discovered the grocery store only had frozen. I'm pretty sure most grandmothers wouldn't go to such trouble. I love you and wish we lived closer!

To my Grandma Jane, the one who called me "little bird" when I was small because I'd stand in her kitchen with my mouth open waiting for her to drop food in. She is no longer with us, but I know with certainty that if she were she'd be so proud of this cookbook. She would be sitting at my kitchen counter peeling carrots for me and saying, "Oh, Chrissy, I wish I could help more," even though she was of course always helpful. I love you, Grandma. I know you knew it when you were here, but I'll keep saying it even though you're gone. I'll see you again one day.

index